# RUN FIT

Improve your running, finish with a smile

Nick Muxlow

First published in 2021 by Nick Muxlow.



NATIONAL LIBRARY OF AUSTRALIA

A catalogue record for this book is available from the National Library of Australia

ISBN: 978 0 6451440 0 0 (paperback)
978 0 6451440 1 7 (ebook)

Printed in Australia by McPhersons Printing Pty Ltd

Cover & interior layout design by Charlotte Gelin Design

Cover photo by James Knowler Takes Photos

Editing by Carolyn Jackson

**Disclaimer**

*To all the runners I have been fortunate enough
to work with and learn from, and whose dreams I have been
privileged to share…*

*I hope the ideas in this book help you to achieve
your full potential, chase bigger dreams and fall in love with
running that little bit more.*

# CONTENTS


**ACKNOWLEDGEMENTS** 11

**FOREWORD** 13

**INTRODUCTION** 17

Who are you? 18
Is this book for you? 19
The Run Fit Way 20
How do I know all this? 22
How to use this book 23
Why I wrote this book 24

## PART 1 – GETTING STARTED ON RUN FIT

**CHAPTER 1: THE RUN FIT WAY** 27

It's not about the race 27
Running will change your life 28
Why do you run? 31
Running is not training 34
The lesson of the apple tree 35
Conclusion 38

**CHAPTER 2 - RUN FIT PRINCIPLES** **39**
A great race experience is built on great training 40
Structure creates enjoyment 42
Variety is key 44
A performance plateau can be prevented 45
Be an inquisitive runner 46
Train when it matters, race when it counts 47
A map and local knowledge are important for the journey 49
Conclusion 51

PART 2 – BECOMING A RUN FIT RUNNER

**THE RUN FIT SCORECARD** **56**

**CHAPTER 3 - GAME PLAN** **57**
Slow and steady wins the race 58
Strategy 60
Deliberate practice 64
Training and racing plans 67
Conclusion 73

**CHAPTER 4 - MINDSET** **75**
You have nothing to fear but fear itself 76
Growth mindset 78
Training mindset 80
Racing mindset 84
Conclusion 87

**CHAPTER 5 - SKILLS** **89**

It's horses for courses 90

Run form 91

Pacing 97

Nutrition and hydration 100

Conclusion 103

**CHAPTER 6 - FITNESS** **105**

There is no magic bullet 107

Develop your endurance 109

Improve your speed 111

Build your strength 114

Conclusion 117

PART 3 – RUN FIT IN ACTION

**CHAPTER 7 - STAYING ON TRACK** **123**

Create good habits 123

How to fit running into your life 125

An ounce of prevention 127

Run load – the key to safe training 129

When prevention is not enough 133

Recovery is part of the plan 134

Conclusion 135

**CHAPTER 8 - RUN FIT COACHING** **137**

The runner's progression 137

Why get a coach? 140

But I'm not good enough for a coach 141

Unconscious incompetence to conscious competence 142

The 1% rule 143

What to expect from coaching 145

The secret ingredients of coaching 147

Conclusion 148

**GET RUN FIT** **149**

**NEXT STEPS** **151**

The Run Fit Scorecard 151

The Run Fit Workshop 151

The Run Fit Club 151

Run Fit personal online coaching – want to be coached by me? 154

**TESTIMONIALS** **155**

Karen Heath 155

Russ Hannah – 100 km ultramarathon runner 155

Marcus Staker – Ultra Trail Australia Silver Buckle holder and miler 156

**A REQUEST** **157**

**ABOUT THE AUTHOR** **159**

# ACKNOWLEDGEMENTS

To all the great coaches, teachers, mentors and wonderful individuals who have had a profound influence on me in all my endeavours: You have all taught me, inspired me and helped shape my views. You have allowed me to become the coach and educator that I am and allowed me to achieve my impossible. Some of you will read this and say, 'Is this me?' It certainly is.

To the team of professionals that has helped keep me on the field, road and trail over the years: You have always been so generous in sharing your knowledge and expertise with me. This is appreciated far more than you have ever realised and, equally, has helped far more than you know.

To all the athletes I have ever been fortunate enough to coach and assist on their personal journeys: It is a privilege to be able to work with such an inspiring and fantastic group of people every day.

To Mum, Dad and Benjamin: Thank you for everything. You are always there to support, encourage and assist however you can in my endless adventures. Never saying 'no', you taught me to dream big, believe in myself and go for it.

To Amber: I look forward to running in the forest with you today and every day. Thank you for pushing me, challenging me and being patient with me, while allowing me to follow my heart in all that I do.

# FOREWORD

When Nick Muxlow contacted me out of the blue to write a Foreword for his latest book, I have to admit that I had no idea who he was. But I always like to help out a fellow runner, so I told him to send along the manuscript and I'd take a look. Well, I have to say that I liked what I saw right off the bat. I loved the subtitle – 'Improve your running … finish with a smile!' Is there a better way to finish a race? Then I opened the book and started to read, and found that I kept nodding, agreeing with Nick and saying 'YES!' out loud over and over again. Run Fit is a book not just for you, but a book that can be shared and discussed as we spread the word to allow runners out there to reach their full potential.

Nick covers many crucial elements for a successful and enjoyable running experience on the way to becoming Run Fit. Much of what he talks about are the theories and practices that I use myself when coaching. He knows that it's all about having the right training processes for you. As the saying goes, 'It is all about the journey, NOT the destination.' This book certainly addresses that by setting out the steps in training to allow you to enjoy your running, but also to be the best at it that you can be. Nick delivers the crucial message that patience and long-term, sustained training practices lead to gradual improvement and, ultimately, success. But Run Fit is about so much more than the physical side of training. It also asks questions to make you think about your life in running … this thought-provoking method ensures you own the training and know why you train the way you do; putting the focus fair and squarely on the outcomes you are striving for.

If I were to make a daily calendar of inspirational quotes to live by, it would read a lot like the topics in Run Fit:

Good training leads to good racing

Structure creates enjoyment

Be an inquisitive runner … have a training plan
that tells you HOW to train rather than just WHAT to do

Train when it matters, race when it counts

Slow and steady wins the race

You have nothing to fear but fear itself

Focus on what matters

In addition to all this inspiration, the book also discusses well constructed training plans and carefully considered methods to ensure you run your best race. Then there is a detailed section on developing your running skill set that is practical, detailed and on point. And just as importantly, there are ways to focus your mind to succeed – an area often not given the attention that I believe it deserves.

I certainly learnt a lot from Nick's wise words and I know you will too. So enjoy the book, learn from it, and I will see you on the start line at an event soon – because I might not see you at the finish line if you adopt the Run Fit way!

*Yours in running.*
*Steve Moneghetti AM*

# INTRODUCTION

All around the world you will find many different kinds of runners. And some of them are Run Fit runners.

Run Fit runners are the ones who improve their running and finish with a smile. They train with confidence, clarity and focus. They are injury free, and they love the process of training and the structure it brings to their life. They have confidence in what they are doing. They thrive on the experiences that training for, competing in and finishing various events allows them to have. They love the challenge and journey of training and are driven to improve. On the start line of a race, they have certainty – certainty that they're going to have a fantastic experience and enjoy the day out. They cross the finish line with a smile, having achieved a new PB, and are already dreaming of their next running adventure. Running brings them abundant happiness. In fact, running is their way of life. We call these people Run Fit runners.

I am endurance coach at The Run Journey, The Ultra Journey and The Kona Journey. I know running and have been a runner all my life. It started with playing chasey and running laps in the schoolyard and progressed to playing centre in my beloved childhood game of lacrosse. From there I moved on to a crazy sport called triathlon, and then to Ironman triathlon. I have now come full circle and am back to pure running. Road, trail and ultramarathon running.

But while I have always been a runner, I have not always been a Run Fit runner. My early attempts at what I thought was run training lacked the clarity, focus and certainty that I now have. The improvement in my running was far slower than it could have been because the critical elements required for a runner to reach their full potential were missing. My mental game was lacking. I didn't make the best use of the time I spent training. I had no long-term plan in place, focusing instead on the here and now. I didn't spend the time I should have refining my skills, preferring instead to compete and believing that was the best and fastest way to improve. I feel like those were wasted years. Years that I could have spent on a consistent path of improvement if I had known in the beginning what I know now.

That knowledge was hard won. I had to seek mentors and coaches and go through the difficult process of trial and error to uncover the fact that there is a better way to do things. This understanding was intensified when I became a running coach. What looked like disorganised progression suddenly became clear. A logical path that runners progress along to improve. A progression that, by putting the right stepping-stones in place at the right time, could be fast-tracked. Ultimately, consistent progression and a love of running, and the process, can be fostered in all. That is the journey that we are going to take you on. If you want to join us…

## WHO ARE YOU?

If you picked up this book, you are undoubtedly a runner, and you probably have a running goal in mind. It might be a 10 km or a half marathon fun run, or you might be eyeing off a marathon. You might be looking to up your game in your chosen event and hit a new PB.

On the other hand, there are runners looking to take things further and tackle a 50 km or 100 km ultramarathon or even dreaming of completing 100 miles. But you all have one thing in common; you are not sure how to reach your goal or what is needed to allow you to be successful in your chosen event. And while there may seem to be vast differences between these events and these types of runners and their level of experience, when we draw together the similarities and understand the process of running we see how much we are alike.

Beyond running in, or wanting to run in, organised events, there is something special that you all have in common – your drive to improve and your love of running. When you started running the improvement came easily, but that has now slowed, and you want to find ways for it to continue. You want to escape the plateau or form slump you're in. You want to understand what you're doing and be able to apply sound training principles to what you do. This brings confidence and certainty, both in your training and when you compete. And while your chosen goal event is important, there is something much deeper pulling you along. Running is your lifestyle. It keeps you fit, it allows you to grow, it challenges you. It's your special thing.

## IS THIS BOOK FOR YOU?

This book is for someone who has been running for a while but does not have a structured training program in place, is currently injured or has been injured regularly in the past, is in a performance plateau (has not set a PB in twelve months) or does not have a lot of variety in their training.

This book is also for people who are keen to really improve their running. They're transitioning from running for exercise to wanting to properly train. At this point there is a mindset shift; they want to improve what they do, but they're often new to the idea of running as training.

This book is also written for the intermediate runner looking to continue their improvement. They have the basics in place, but this structure lacks clarity and cohesion, and parts are missing. They don't quite understand how it all comes together. In both instances, these runners are seeking certainty on how to train so they can train with confidence and improve their running.

If you're one of these runners, you probably have a lot of questions. As a coach, I'm used to getting a lot of questions. How do I improve my run form? What do I need to eat and drink? How do I improve my fitness? Do I need to do strength training? What's the best training plan to follow? What's your favourite run set? How do I prevent cramping? How many miles can I run in a week? How do I build my distance? I don't think I'm going to make the distance, what do you suggest? How can I improve my run speed? I'm injured all the time, can you help?

All these questions can be summed up in one pivotal question: How do I get Run Fit?

## THE RUN FIT WAY

Run Fit is simultaneously a noun, a verb, and an adjective:

- Run Fit is an idea

- Run Fit is something you do
- Run Fit is a way to describe a particular individual

Run Fit runners train with confidence, improve their running, enjoy the journey and finish with a smile.

It won't be difficult to become a Run Fit runner in the next six to twelve months if you put in place the ideas, concepts and method that I talk about in this book. It becomes your guiding light, your path to derive motivation, meaning and purpose from your running.

There is a lot to worry about when it comes to running, and so we need a clear and logical process to follow. Something to order our thinking and ensure we are not forgetting something or leaving something out. Enter the Run Fit Way, which is laid out in the following pages.

We will start by diving into the Run Fit philosophy in more depth to ground your understanding. Following this, we will look at the key guiding principles required for you to shift your mindset and be open to becoming Run Fit. This will be the point at which we are ready to jump into the Run Fit Method. A method to make sure we achieve our goal of becoming Run Fit. There are four parts to the method:

- Game Plan,
- Mindset,
- Skills; and
- Fitness.

All are required for you to become Run Fit.

After unpacking this process and putting a glorious structure in place for your running, we will look at the Run Fit Way in action, including vital information on avoiding injuries, and what to expect from Run Fit Coaching. By the end of this book you will have the knowledge to be a Run Fit runner, and will already be implementing the ideas to ensure you *become* a Run Fit runner.

## HOW DO I KNOW ALL THIS?

As I said earlier, I have been a runner all my life. But being a good runner does not make you a great coach or allow you the understanding to help others achieve their full human potential. My other passion, coaching, is underpinned by a Bachelor of Applied Science Human Movement (Exercise and Sports Science) and a Bachelor of Education. I have been a coach for twenty years, and I'm the author of *Journey to 100* and *Journey to Kona*. I have been fortunate to be featured in industry publications, speak regularly to endurance athletes and professional associations, and am known for helping runners to improve their times by 20–60 minutes, train with confidence, enjoy the journey and finish with a smile. A lot of what we are going to unpack over the coming pages.

My personal accomplishments are as varied as the running I love. They include winning the state trail championships, the state ultramarathon championships, and running a 100 km ultra in the Blue Mountains where I received the highly sought after silver belt buckle. My marathon PB is 2 hours, 45 minutes, and I have represented Australia in multiple triathlon races and also finished the ultimate race – the Hawaii Ironman World Championships.

But above all this stand the achievements of the runners I am fortunate to coach. All the runners I coach inspire me. Some you will hear about in this book. It might be the runner who is just beginning and has completed their first 5 km event before progressing to the 10 km and half marathon. Or the runners who decided to step up from the marathon and embark upon a 50 km adventure or a 100 km epic. Then there is the 100 km runner who gained his silver belt buckle when he finished Ultra Trail Australia in under fourteen hours, smashing his PB by over an hour to make his dream a reality. Each and every runner has something they're running for which is meaningful to them. They push themselves, challenge themselves, improve, and do it all again, loving every step of their journey. You soon will have your own stories to tell about your running journey and how you improved and reached your full human potential. That is the journey you are about to embark upon.

## HOW TO USE THIS BOOK

This book wasn't written just to be read. It was written to be highlighted, written in, referred to, shared and discussed.

Reading the book will give you a basic level of understanding. However, to drive forward your knowledge and understanding of the concepts presented, we recommend *engrossing* yourself in the book. I give you permission to highlight sentences, tab pages, mark it and write in it. Highlight the important points so that you can refer back to them, and fill out the exercises in the book – no need to get another piece of paper. This is *your* book to improve *your* running.

You will find exercises throughout the book designed to help unpack your thinking and improve your running. These are entitled 'Your

Journey'. Don't be passive in this process. The exercises are never hard or long but will require thought – they are your cue to take action.

Share the book with other runners. Talk about the concepts it presents when you're out on a run. This will develop your understanding further, make it more enjoyable as you implement the concepts alongside someone else, or give you something new and fresh to talk about and clarify your thinking. You may be forced to re-read or look back over a section (those highlighted bits) to solidify your understanding. To help, I have included questions you can talk about and discuss when on the run under the heading 'On the Run'. I did say – this book was written so you can take action.

## WHY I WROTE THIS BOOK

While I love running and coaching, there is something deeper that drives me. I love to help people achieve their full human potential. Everything I do comes back to this central idea: either me pushing towards my full potential or helping others to push towards theirs. This book is no different. It exists to allow runners to push towards their full human potential. To see what they are capable of and transfer the knowledge and skills they learn in running to everyday life. This allows them to achieve even bigger dreams in both their running *and* their life.

People all over the world enjoy being a Run Fit runner through unlocking the clarity and focus that a proven method brings. We are going to unlock and discuss that method in the coming pages.

If you are ready to be a Run Fit runner, read on.

**PART 1**

# GETTING STARTED ON RUN FIT

As runners, we need to appreciate why we run. Far too many runners don't take the time to unpack the reasons why they run or what they hope to get out of running. They stumble along without making logical decisions about what they want to achieve over the long term. But we will solve this problem.

Part 1 looks at how running can change your life and helps you investigate what running means to you. This clarity will help you make appropriate training decisions in the future. With this understanding in place, we will embark upon developing our understanding around the many principles that underpin a sound running program and also unpack the often-misunderstood difference between running and training. We will finish by ensuring you understand where you want to go with your training and why it's important to have a map and a guide on how to get there.

CHAPTER 1

# THE RUN FIT WAY

*Running is more than a race*

The Run Fit Way starts by understanding a set of core beliefs about why you run and what running means to you. From here we progress to understanding how running can affect our lives and where racing fits into the equation. We then look at the difference between exercising and training, and why truly training will give you a more profound experience than just running. And there's also a lesson to be learned from the apple orchard. Let's get started.

## IT'S NOT ABOUT THE RACE

If you think it's about the race, you have missed the point. The race is part of a much bigger picture. If we consider the time spent in training compared to the time spent competing in or completing an event, this *has* to be the case. You may spend as long as twenty-four weeks preparing for a key event, with some minor races along the way. If we add up all the time spent in training and contrast this with the time taken to run the event you're training for, that race is nothing but a brief flash that is quickly over. On top of that, you may spend years running and improving to reach your full potential. So it must be about something else – something more than winning or finishing a race. It's a cliché to say that happiness is the journey, not the destination, but clichés are often true.

While it must be about the journey, far too many runners are not aware of this. They focus all their effort on the event they're training for and fail to embrace the journey that is taking them there. They bounce from one event to another, without pause or reflection or consideration for what they're doing in between. Always wanting to run faster or stronger, but never changing what they do. Fostering a love of the *process* of improving your running is the way forward. It is not only in the event that you grow; it is through the training. This is more likely to happen when the training is structured and well thought out. If we can appreciate that we are on a journey and learn to love this journey as well as the event, then we have a winning combination. To do this, you need to understand the deeper meaning behind why you run.

## RUNNING WILL CHANGE YOUR LIFE

'Why run?' … 'Because it will change your life!'

'Why run?' is a question that runners are often asked. The answer 'Because it will change your life' is simple, profound and true. Even if it does produce some quizzical looks. Aren't they priceless? But few people will ever understand the power of this statement, because for true understanding you have to take the journey yourself. You have to build up and commit to the process of achieving something you have never achieved before. Let's dive a little deeper and look at why running changes your life.

Running and preparing for a challenging event you have never competed in, or achieving something you have never achieved before, is so much more than 'simply' running. Preparing and training for your first half marathon or marathon is huge. From there, the step up to the 50 km or 100 km ultra is massive. Then you have another leap if you set your sights on the 100 mile event. Whether you're looking at your first half marathon or first 100 miler, the adventure will push you further than you ever thought physically possible and further than you ever thought mentally possible. It teaches you who you really are and what you are capable of.

This kind of adventure is absolutely not for the faint-hearted. If it were, everyone would be doing it. But that's the point. Not everyone is doing it because not everyone is prepared to step outside their comfort zone; they're too scared to commit to such a life-changing experience. They listen to the little voice in their head that doubts their ability. They listen to others who doubt their ability. They're listening to the wrong voices. They need to listen to the little echo that does believe they can do it. That echo can be hard to hear, but it is there – deep inside them, the glimmer of belief is real.

When you do commit and commit fully, the journey of building up to achieve something you have never achieved before changes your life in real and often unexpected ways. This is because when you begin the journey of running to achieve your personal goals, you are saying to the world, your friends and family, 'I'm prepared to embark upon something that is outside my comfort zone. It scares me, yes, there is fear, but I'm going to accept it, I'm going to go for it, I'm going to commit.'

You can't run and not change. But you may be wondering what these 'magical' changes are that we're talking about. Running teaches you dedication, commitment, focus and clarity. It teaches you to believe in yourself. If you don't believe me, ask any runner who has completed a race or achieved a PB that caused them to step outside their comfort zone. Ask them to reflect whether running affected them in the ways I've described. They will certainly agree that it has.

How does running do this? To start, you have to learn to put small, meaningful steps in place over a long period to be able to achieve your goal. This requires planning and daily commitment. It therefore teaches you to prioritise and create good habits. Suddenly you learn what is truly important in your life and what is not. TV time decreases, social media time decreases, stress reduces, exercise time increases and time spent in nature increases. Time spent with friends also increases, and more importantly becomes more meaningful as you spend quality time running with friends who have similar values. Family time increases as you find ways to include your family on your journey.

When you run you learn to follow a plan. You learn about the power of committing to the big things in life. Not the small, trivial things that waste your time and won't matter in time. By achieving your goal you prove to yourself that you are capable and can achieve things that you once never thought possible. You now have an experience to prove it. The challenge and adventure you face shifts your 'yardstick'. Now, every challenge or problem you face in life is measured against a new norm. Achieving your goal gives you clarity on how to tackle these other challenges; no longer is anything impossible. Running is a catalyst for everything else you want to achieve in life.

If you're ready to change your life, don't be put off by the fear and doubts in your mind. Block out the insecurity of others who don't understand and make the jump. Commit to your goals and put in place a plan and people who can help you get there. Are you a thinker or a doer? A wannabe or an action taker? A coulda' or a committer? Go on, commit. You'll look back in twelve months' time and be glad that you did.

Let's now look at why you run, and the goals you want to achieve that you have never dreamed of achieving before.

## WHY DO YOU RUN?

What are the reasons you run? Different people run for different reasons and often for more than one reason. Some people run for fitness, others for the challenge. There are people who run to connect to nature because they spend all day in an office and can't wait to get out among the trees. Some run to de-stress and to think things over. Others run because it pushes their mindset – everything in their life is easy and comfortable, so they love long races that cause discomfort, pain and suffering. They feel that on the other side of this discomfort they grow and learn what is meaningful in life. Others run for the adventure – running to far away places, running to where they have never been before, running to see things they have never seen before. Some runners run for the camaraderie and the friendship. Their running is their way of being social. They talk to their running buddies to organise their running, they talk to their friends while they're running, they talk over coffee after running. Others love the structure that running brings to their life and thrive on this.

Others simply run for the fun.

People run for many and varied reasons. It's helpful to have insight and understand your reasons for running, as this provides clarity in your thinking and decision making moving forward. It also helps you build experiences to enhance and foster this love.

So let's ask the question, 'Why do you run?'

## YOUR JOURNEY

List the reasons why you run below. Aim for five or more.

1. Fitness
2. challenge
3. Destress + structure
4. – would enjoy the social aspect at some point –
5. Run a marathon.

## ON THE RUN

Ask your running partner why they run.

I love to share the gorgeous story of the first runner I coached. Amy came to me with one intention: to run the New York Marathon. I can distinctly remember her saying words to the effect of, 'I want to train for the New York Marathon, that is it.' I reassured her that this was fine, and we would make sure she could finish the New York Marathon, have fun and love the experience. She was in. She progressed beautifully, gradually building the distance of her runs, increasing her knowledge and improving her running skills. She completed a few other races along the way, and then she was off to America. Amy ran the New York Marathon and had a blast.

As I had never coached a runner to the New York Marathon before (little did Amy know, I had never coached a runner at all at that stage), I wanted to know how it went and hear more about the event. I love to talk about running and wanted to know about her experience, and we had a lovely chat. But afterwards she gave me the surprise of my life. I said that Amy had come to me with a specific goal, and nothing more, so you can imagine my shock when she said, 'Nick, I know I said I only wanted to run New York, but now I want to run the Dopey Challenge.' I nearly fell off my chair. The Dopey Challenge is the pinnacle of the Walt Disney World Marathon Weekend. It consists of running 5 km on Thursday, 10 km on Friday, a half marathon on Saturday and a full marathon on Sunday. A glorious 78.3 km of running over four days. Each run is completed early in the morning before the theme parks open, so competitors can spend the rest of the day walking around enjoying the parks.

After I straightened myself up on my chair, I replied, 'Sure, you'll be able to achieve that.' Amy had wanted to run the New York Marathon for the challenge and the fun of the experience, but through that experience she learned to love running. She wanted to continue running because of the structure that it brought to her life, and to challenge herself by setting bigger and bigger goals. She loved the fun of preparing for and competing in events and the experiences that it brought her. Amy is a Run Fit runner and still loves her running to this day.

## RUNNING IS NOT TRAINING

There is a difference between going out for a run and training. It's when you begin to train that running truly has the power to change your life.

Going out for a run can be a great form of exercise. This is when you go out running without a goal to work towards or a focus for what you're doing. The purpose behind your run is normally to keep fit, but may also include de-stressing and connecting with nature.

Training is when you put in place specific, targeted and meaningful steps at particular times to progress different aspects of your knowledge, mindset, skills or fitness for a desired outcome. This outcome is normally an improvement in your ability with respect to an event you're working towards. In other words, you are running with a specific focus. Normally the event you're working towards is an opportunity to achieve something you have never achieved before.

Running in this way allows you to obtain the benefits of exercising, de-stressing and connecting with nature, but has the additional benefits of challenging you, improving your fitness in a targeted way, and allowing you to improve as a runner as you progress through your training program.

While running for exercise is certainly fantastic and we are all for that, far too often we find runners wanting to undertake run training who are just exercising, or simply going out for a run. These runners may improve for a while, but this improvement soon stops and they hit a performance plateau. On the other hand, the person who is training, as opposed to just running, continues to improve, has focus and clarity with what they're doing, and loves the journey. As we progress, we will outline a process to ensure you are training when you go running and able to enjoy all the benefits running has to offer.

When your running becomes training and you are able shoot for those life-changing goals, you will be a Run Fit runner.

## THE LESSON OF THE APPLE TREE

I want you to be ambitious, but I also want you to be patient. Let's consider what an apple tree can teach us about becoming a better runner.

The farmer doesn't plant an apple tree and expect to eat apples the following year. At first, the branches are weak, the roots delicate. The tree is unable to support the apples. The farmer needs to care for the tree. The farmer needs to protect it from the damage of heat, wind, drought and driving rain.

The farmer needs to water the tree regularly while it's young, fertilise it, and provide it with support to allow it to grow big, strong and healthy. As the tree grows the apples go from being small, sour and scarce to large, delicious and plentiful.

The farmer doesn't rush the growing process because they know that the more love, time and attention they put in, the juicier the fruit will be. They know that, in the long term, the care and time taken are a sound investment in the rewards they seek.

Your running is no different. Your body is no different.

When you're a young runner you need to develop, grow and be careful of your delicate body. As you progress, you become better able to tolerate the stresses of a running life. You become a stronger, more powerful and faster runner.

But even when you are strong, powerful and fast, you will need to take care. The apple tree always needs care, but when this care is taken the fruit is always plentiful.

Are you trying to rush the process of becoming a strong apple tree?

Far too often runners are focused on the short term. Next week's parkrun,[1] the half marathon that's seven weeks off, their next marathon. They don't slow down and put the right building blocks in place at the right time with respect to their long-term goals. They're caught in the here and now without taking a step back and looking at the bigger picture of where they want to go. Take a deep breath and consider where you want to go with your running.

## YOUR JOURNEY

Where would you like to be with your running in six months, one year, three years and a lifetime from now? Consider what events you would like to run, what experiences you would like to have, what running trips, holidays or runcations you would like to go on. Where locally, interstate and internationally will you have run by that time? Which cities will you have run in? Boston, Berlin, London, Tokyo, Paris, Sydney? What environments will you have run in? The jungle, the desert, the snow, the mountains? What friendships or groups will you belong to, and who will you run with?

1 A weekly 5 km running event held in parks throughout the world.

In six months?

- half marathon.

In one year?

- marathon.

In three years?

- Disney run.

What experiences would you like to have with your running?

Over your lifetime, what would you like to achieve in running?

- running partner

## ON THE RUN

Ask your run partner(s) the same questions I asked you. Where would you like to be with your running in six months, one year, three years or a lifetime? What other fun and exciting run experiences or run adventures can you come up with together?

## CONCLUSION

You now have an appreciation that running will change your life through the parallel growth it allows in your life away from running. You have progressed to understand that we must focus on the journey, not just the destination. You have unpacked why you run and have written down everything that you would like to achieve run-wise, both with races and run experiences, for specific milestones and over a lifetime. You know the difference between running for exercise and training, and are aware that to improve you must include run training in what you do. Simply going out for 'a run' all the time won't cut it. Finally, you understand and acknowledge that you must take care of your body and build it to be strong and capable of coping with the demands of running. If you do this, it will provide an abundance of love and reward you by allowing you to achieve all your running goals.

CHAPTER 2

# RUN FIT PRINCIPLES

*The experience you have in your race depends on the quality of your training*

To be Run Fit requires a background understanding of the key principles which underpin the method. We are going to launch into sharing these guiding principles with you now. While I know you are dying to get straight to the method, it will make better sense if we understand the concepts that underpin it. I am known for being massive on the 'Why', and there is a reason for that – we need this understanding for you to fully transform into a Run Fit runner.

In this chapter we are going to look at some key concepts. We will look at why the experience you have on race day depends on the quality of your training. Then we will cover how structure brings enjoyment to your training and why variety is important. Next we will help you understand how you actually improve your running – by being an inquisitive runner. Then we will discuss how a plateau in performance can be avoided, and why you must train when it matters and race when it counts.

With these key principles under your belt, you will be primed to jump in and unpack the Run Fit Method in Part 2. Let's get to it.

## A GREAT RACE EXPERIENCE IS BUILT ON GREAT TRAINING

The experience you have on race day depends on the quality of your training. If you haven't prepared correctly for your event – and that's any event from a 5 km to an ultramarathon – then it makes it very difficult, even impossible, to execute a great race. Far too often, however, runners undertake training that is unsuited to their goal event. Depending on where someone is at with their understanding of run training principles, it may be that they don't run enough, or they don't run hard enough, or they do all their running too hard. The mistake runners often make is that they just front up at the start line of their event, expecting to run a great time and have a great time, without having undertaken a quality training program. They simply think that whatever running they have done will do the trick. But this is simply not the case. We need to improve our training to improve both how we run in an event and the experience we have.

The next mistake runners make with their training is that they 'just go and run'. Just going for a run is not making the most effective use of your time to get the result you desire in your chosen event. We discussed in Chapter 1 that simply 'going for a run' is not training, but this goes further. Within your training we need to build your skill set to ensure you have the expertise you need to have a great race; we need to build your fitness to ensure you can last the distance at your desired pace; and we need to build your experience – that is, ensure you have tackled in training many of the challenges that you will face in the race – so that you are prepared for anything. These are all required to ensure you have a great race.

Whenever I start working with a runner I ask the question: What knowledge, skills and experience do they need to give them an exceptional race and a wonderful experience? What is the knowledge, skill set and understanding you need to move from where you are now, progress through your training and ultimately finish with a smile?

## YOUR JOURNEY

What knowledge do you need to have a great race? List it all below in bullet points.

-
-

What skills do you need to have a great race? List them all below in bullet points.

-
-

What experience do you need to have a great race? List it all below in bullet points.

-
-

## ON THE RUN

Ask your run partner the questions above. What do they come up with? How were their answers similar to yours and how were they different? Do you need to add anything to your list?

The intention of this exercise is to discover two things. Firstly, are you building into your run training plan all the areas you need to develop or work on that you identified on page 41? Secondly, do you know what is missing?

There is a particular challenge that a runner faces when pushing their comfort zones to achieve something they have never achieved before. Which is that if you have not been there before, you won't know what needs to be done to get there. But you're reading this book, which is a great start. So, if your list looks minimal, that is okay, because you can't know what you don't know. And that's where I step in as your running coach.

In Part 2 we will look in more detail at exactly what makes a quality training program, but meanwhile stay with me as we explain a few more mission critical ideas.

## STRUCTURE CREATES ENJOYMENT

Bringing structure to running increases the enjoyment runners have. Structure is essential for successful run improvement. It helps create positive run habits and allows gradual progression of the training sets. Runners typically start by running when they can, which is great. But this can lead to weeks when there is lots of running happening and weeks when there is limited running or no running happening. It also typically results in lots of running immediately before a goal race. Which is not necessarily a good thing.

When we bring a structured run program to a runner, they thrive on it. Structure brings enjoyment. It does this by making sure runners don't waste mental energy ruminating over their training and wondering if they should run that day, how far, or indeed what else they should do. They know that if they have a structured run plan, all the progression has been taken care of and all the deliberate practice has been embedded in it. In essence, all the thinking has been done for them and all they have to do is follow the plan. They know when they have to train and what they have to do within each and every run set. They run with confidence and can be certain that they will improve. This creates long-term consistency with their running, which is essential for improvement. Long-term, gradual progression always wins.

There are many options when it comes to structuring a training plan. Many runners work on a weekly structure of harder runs on Tuesday and Thursday with a long run on Sunday when they have more time. But there are of course other options. This base structure can be changed if parents have to take kids to sport on the weekend, but have a half or full day off during the week. They could schedule hard runs on Mondays and Wednesdays and a long run on the Friday. Additional supporting runs, strength sets and recovery practices can be included around these key runs. There is an endless list of possibilities for structuring a run training program. The key here is that when you have a structured training program that works with your personal circumstances, you will enjoy your training more because you aren't continually trying to juggle competing demands.

What we are doing here is bringing in a process for runners to follow. I am regularly heard saying to runners, 'Follow the process to progress.' It is blocks of training that will deliver results; there is no magic set. Confidence comes from having a training plan.

## VARIETY IS KEY

With a structure in place we can look to increase the variety of what you do. If you complete the same run set, day in day out, over the same course or at the same location, you will get bored very quickly. This leads to burnout and mental exhaustion, which is the opposite of what we want to achieve. We want to create excitement, adventure and fun with your running, and variety allows this. Once again, just saying 'I'm going out for a run' won't cut it.

You have endless variety that can be undertaken with your running. You can do interval sets, fartlek runs, tempo runs, threshold sets, ramp runs, pyramid sets, build runs or progressive runs. You can do uphill efforts, pacing sets, nutrition sets, long runs as well as the beloved steady aerobic run. We can do runs based on heart rate, effort and power. Variety in your running is essential – for both the physical and mental advantages it gives you – and with so many options to choose from, it's easy to change the sets that you're running each week and within the week.

Beyond this we can look to change the style of running depending on the season. You could go short and fast (5 km and 10 km) over the summer, and undertake long, half and full marathon running over the winter. You could target a half marathon over the summer and move to trail running over winter or, my personal favourite, tackle the road and marathon running over summer and then the ultramarathon running over winter.

We can also change the style of running for different times of the year. For instance, after the last major event or race of the season and after some recovery time, I use a lot of RPE sets and fartlek sets with runners. Runners find these mentally easier than many of the other sets, and such an approach allows long-term running consistency without mental burnout.

### A PERFORMANCE PLATEAU CAN BE PREVENTED

A further reason for bringing structure and variety to your running is to help you avoid a plateau in your performance. Hitting a plateau in performance is a common problem among runners. If you get caught completing the same runs week in and week out, your run load becomes very stagnant, and this stagnation leads to a plateau. In fact it is not unusual for me to see runners completing the same training year on year, then wondering why they're making the same mistakes each year or failing to improve. But as Einstein said, the definition of insanity is doing the same thing over and over and expecting different results.

While it may seem obvious when put like this, it is not obvious for the runner. They feel like they are changing up their training because they change the distance they're running. But just running further is not the same as fundamentally changing what they do in the run sets – and this is what counts. They are completing the same training over and over without understanding what they're doing. As a result, they continue to get lousy results. The bit which astounds me is that they don't make a change. Don't let this be you. Make positive changes in your run training, and learn how to train so you can improve your results.

The best way to avoid hitting a plateau in performance is to use what coaches like to call periodization (the long-term structure of a training plan) to your advantage. Using such an approach is beneficial because it ensures that you are in peak physical and mental condition for key events. This means that you race fast when it matters. Periodization also ensures that there are periods of rest, recovery and renewal. This allows you to mentally and physically recharge at appropriate times and be ready for focused training and big events in the future.

While it is beneficial to run year-round, the aspect of your running that you choose to develop, the focus of your run sets, and the structure within the sets needs to change and become more specific as your event approaches.

## BE AN INQUISITIVE RUNNER

Through a well-structured and detailed training program, we are able to teach you *how* to train. This is a very different approach from the coaches and run plans that simply tell you *what* to do. For such an approach to work, you have to be inquisitive. You have to be looking at your program and asking yourself, 'Why are we doing this?' We want you to understand *why* you are doing what we ask you to do. If you understand why you're doing something, then you become invested in the process and understand what you are trying to improve as opposed to simply doing it because you have to. When you can see the reason why you need to do something, you will be far more motivated. You will see the connection between your actions and their outcomes.

By teaching you how to train, we build knowledge and skills that stay with you for life. While you may not execute every race perfectly, or run every set perfectly, this becomes part of the progression, part of your journey. You finish training sets and races and are not left with questions about why things didn't go to plan; you already understand why because you have the knowledge. You are left with the ability to improve the set next time you complete it. Improve elements of your race next time around. You are empowered to take a growth mindset to your running and unlock continuous improvement.

## TRAIN WHEN IT MATTERS, RACE WHEN IT COUNTS

We don't want you to race all the time. Racing all the time is fraught with danger. It undermines your training and your racing. Racing all the time occurs in two main ways. The first is when runners look to race in each and every run they do. Whenever they head out the door, it's a race; a run in which they push themselves as hard as they can. It also occurs when runners choose to race the same set each week and hope to set a PB each and every time.

The classic example of this occurs at parkrun. Runners typically start competing in structured events with parkrun, and are really excited to finish 5 km for the first time. This progresses to wanting to run the whole way. Once this is achieved, they have started to develop from a social runner into a competitive runner (even if they only compete against themselves). This is awesome, but the next thing that generally occurs is the PB streak. They now want to set a PB. They run the race harder and harder each week. This works initially, and they set PB after PB. Then suddenly a plateau happens.

The PBs become sporadic, happening every now and again. This is when the new runner often loses heart. It doesn't seem as easy any more, and they start to doubt themselves and beat themselves up. What they don't realise is that their body simply doesn't adapt that quickly. They don't know what is required to race really well so that they can continue to set PBs after this initial streak. What we need to do is improve our training, as this will improve our racing.

You need to understand two key points here: that the body doesn't adapt that quickly to training, and that racing requires an extra special effort. You need to be mentally prepared for a big race, and we need to decrease your training prior to competing. This is known as a taper. What is also often overlooked is that you should not undertake your usual training the week after a big race. We are going to have to have some recovery time. This might be a day or two after a shorter race, a few days for a 10–12 km fun run, right up to a week or two after a 100 km ultramarathon. This recovery period will also look different for different runners. A new runner might have days entirely free of running, while a more experienced runner might complete a few days of easier running.

The take-away from all of this is that we need to train when it matters and race when it counts. You need to train for the results that you care about. If you're keen to set a 5 km PB at parkrun or another event, that is absolutely fantastic, but we need to put the training in to allow it to happen and make certain it happens. We can then race when it counts. We can progress your training and develop a program that allows the body to adapt well physiologically and peak when you have a race. At this point you can race your heart out, because it counts. Never forget that you should: train when it matters, race when it counts.

## A MAP AND LOCAL KNOWLEDGE ARE IMPORTANT FOR THE JOURNEY

In Part 2 we are going to launch into the Run Fit Method. But before we get to this there is one final idea that we need to unpack. While we discovered why you run in Chapter 1, we have not yet looked at the concept of where you are now and where you want to be.

First, we need to give you an anchoring experience by undertaking the following exercise.

### YOUR JOURNEY

What have you achieved in the past that has had significance and meaning for you? This can be running related, but doesn't have to be – it can be something that has nothing to with running.

1. 14km race
2. Started w/ a running group
3. Signed up for a half marathon
4.
5.

If you reflect on these achievements, I'll bet that they all required you to work hard and that they pushed you outside your comfort zone, causing you to have to grow as an individual. Your running is no different. To achieve meaning and significance in your running, you are going to have to push yourself outside your comfort zone and work hard for your results. To do anything less will decrease the significance in your own mind of what you achieve. Not by anyone else's standard, but by your own. Embrace the challenge and do the hard work.

Where you are now is point A. Where you want to get to is point B. That point B might be a PB, the furthest you have ever run, a destination race or some other beautiful running adventure. This point B is future related.

Now let's put these two concepts together. We are at point A and we know that we are going to have to undertake some hard work, be dedicated and show commitment to arrive at point B. If this doesn't happen or is not required, the satisfaction and joy we receive at point B will be less than we hoped for.

This is a powerful concept to understand and a lovely understanding to have. Point B can now be wherever we want it to be. We are going to be pushing your comfort zones to achieve something you have never achieved before. But how do we go about this?

If you rocked up in a city you have never been to before and were keen to find the magnificent monument that carries the town's name, you have three options. Stumble around until you find it, ask a local who has been there before and can give you directions, or buy a map – a detailed map that outlines the path you need to take.

I am yet to find anyone who chooses the first option – stumble around until they find the monument. That option is obviously silly, but if that's the case, why do so many runners take a similar approach to their running? They don't put in place a plan or ask others who have been there before how to get there. They start stumbling, as if stumbling around trying to get there is more righteous.

Personally, I think a better approach is to ask someone who knows, get a map, enjoy the journey and arrive at the destination with a smile. Chances are, if you were to take your map but also talk to a local, they would say something along the lines of, 'The monument is here. You can head straight along this road and turn left, but if you really want to experience the city you should turn right up this road, stop off at this restaurant – it's fabulous – head down this street because the view from here is absolutely stunning, and then the monument will be on your left. Enjoy!'

Your running is no different. You need a map and the guidance of a local to allow you to get the most out of your running. That method is what we running coaches call a process. A tried and tested process to get you from your point A to your point B. Enjoying the journey and finishing with a smile.

## CONCLUSION

We have now covered the important principles that underpin the Run Fit Method. You know that a great race experience is built upon great training, and that you must prepare correctly to have the experience that you desire. You appreciate that structure creates enjoyment for the runner and allows positive run habits to be formed and momentum to be built with your running. You understand that variety is key to long-term motivation and understand how we can go about achieving this variety. You are also equipped to ensure you never hit a performance plateau by utilising periodization and ensuring you're in peak physical and mental condition around key events. You also understand how the body adapts and the need for recovery, and so you must train when it matters and race when it counts. Finally, you now appreciate that the best way to get to your destination and have a fantastic experience is to use a map and ask a local for guidance. That map and guidance is your training plan and a coach.

Tighten those laces; you are now primed to launch into the Run Fit Method.

**PART 2**

# BECOMING A RUN FIT RUNNER

The Run Fit Method is a process that you can follow to ensure that all elements required by you, the runner, to become the best runner you can be are developed to their full potential. Often coaches and runners only focus on one or two elements of their running and miss others. Such an approach is scattered and lacks clarity and direction. Essential elements required for you to reach your full human potential are being forgotten. Run Fit is a method that ensures nothing is forgotten. It breaks your running down into the four key areas required for your success. It then details the three key focus points of each area. The method unlocks continuous improvement for you, the runner. It gives you certainty and clarity with your training, allowing you to train with confidence. And above all, it makes sense.

The four parts of the Run Fit Method are:

- Game Plan,
- Mindset,
- Skills; and
- Fitness.

To improve your running, every part of the Run Fit Method is required. If any one part is missing, you may experience problems on the way to your destination.

Now, before we look at each part in depth, let's take a quick overview. The Game Plan is the backbone of the method and allows the concepts covered in Mindset, Skills and Fitness to be implemented and achieved. The Game Plan is what delivers structure to your running. Mindset is about ensuring that you have a positive mindset when both training and racing. Skills looks at the full range of skills needed by the runner: the techniques needed to be successful. Last, but certainly not least, we have Fitness.

To be able to drive your fitness to its full capacity, we need to have implemented the other three parts of the

Run Fit Method. When all four parts come together, you will be able to reach your peak physical and psychological state and, therefore, your full potential as a runner. You will be Run Fit.

Below is a diagram of what this looks like and how all four parts of the method combine to allow you to become Run Fit.

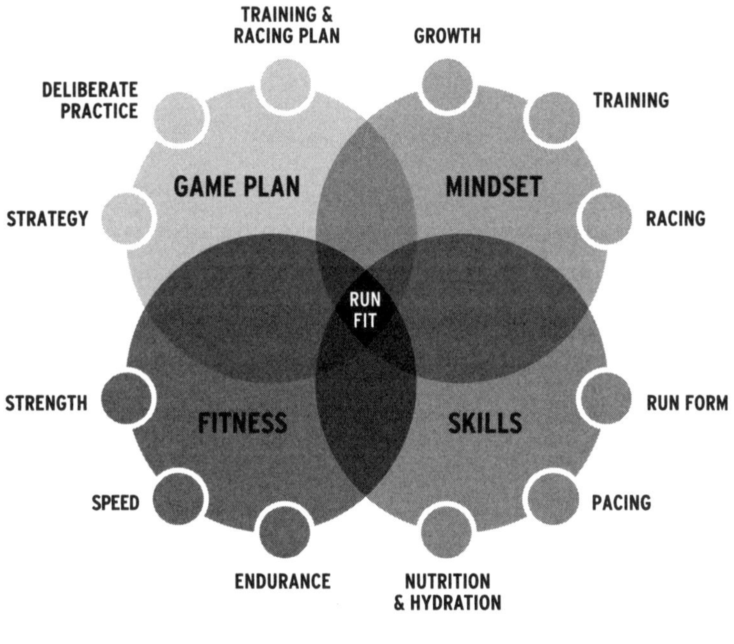

## THE RUN FIT SCORECARD

So where do you start? To find a good starting point with your running we recommend jumping online and taking the Run Fit Scorecard. The scorecard is designed to give you a score in each of the areas that we are about to unpack. By completing the scorecard now you will get a clear idea of where your knowledge is at – a (start) line in the sand. You can then take the scorecard again after reading the following chapters that explain the Run Fit Method. This will let you see how far your understanding has come after just doing a bit of reading. If you don't take the scorecard before reading on, you won't be able to see how much you have already grown.

### YOUR JOURNEY

Take the Run Fit Scorecard. The questions are designed to score you on the four areas required to become Run Fit as described in this book. It gives you a personalised report, which can be used to fast-track your improvement.

Take the scorecard at www.therunjourney.com/scorecard.
It will take 5–10 minutes.

CHAPTER 3

# GAME PLAN

*Long-term gradual progression leads to success*

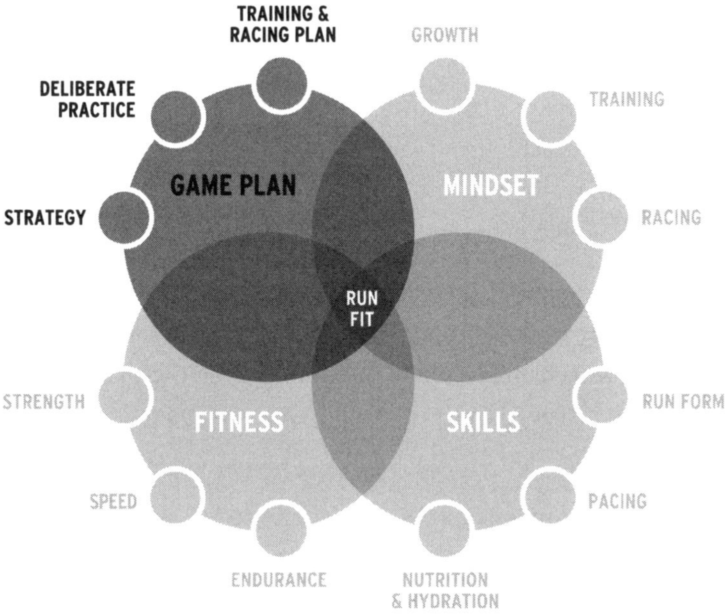


The Game Plan is the backbone of becoming and being Run Fit. It allows everything that follows to be put in place. This is a point I cannot emphasise enough. The Game Plan comprises three main elements:

- A strategy,
- Deliberate practice; and
- A training and racing plan.

The diagram on the previous page shows how these components fit into the Game Plan.

Now, I know you're dying to read about all things running, but before we look at each part of the Game Plan in depth, there's a key concept I want you to understand, which is that…

## SLOW AND STEADY WINS THE RACE

Runners often have a bias towards the short term. They regularly come to me for coaching and say something along the lines of, 'I have been training really well and I want your help over the last twelve weeks leading into my event.'

Sounds simple enough, doesn't it? But what these runners fail to appreciate is that what we can achieve in the last twelve weeks is dependent on what has been put in place in the twelve weeks prior. And what can be achieved in those twelve weeks is often dependent on what has been achieved in the months, years or even a lifetime prior.

They also fail to understand that we often need to take time to build up their skills and knowledge. We will get to this in more depth in Chapter 5, but suffice to say here that we need to *acquire* knowledge before we can *implement* knowledge. Only when we have both will we see results. This process takes time and cannot be fast-tracked. Further, the body takes time to adapt to training, and when we rush we risk injury.

As a runner, you need to get over your bias towards short-term thinking, and understand that long-term, gradual progression is the key to a successful running career.

Long-term, gradual progression means that as a runner you progress different aspects of your running gradually. We may gradually build up the distance or time of your long run, gradually build up the frequency of your running, gradually build up the distance of the events you enter, or gradually build up the time of the intensity efforts you complete.

Let's say we have a runner who has a 30-minute PB for the 5 km (6min/km) who is keen to shift this down to a sub 25-minute time (5min/km). They cannot simply start running hard efforts at the time they hope to achieve and the pace they hope to achieve. It will take gradual progression to allow them to achieve their goal. Slowly, 6min/km becomes 5.55/km, then 5.50/km then 5.40/km, and so on. They need to complete the right training at the right intensity to allow this. If they simply start running harder, they are not allowing their body to adapt and may not be doing the right training to allow them to achieve their desired outcome. If, however, they take the long-term, gradual approach, they will get there. The same concept applies for different runners, races and goals.

I'll illustrate this point by looking at a runner I have coached for a long time. John came to me for coaching leading into his first big event – fortunately about six months out, not twelve weeks! He progressed beautifully; we developed his knowledge of training and put in place the skills he needed. He completed his first race, achieving the goal he had set himself, and crossed the finish line with a smile. But John had bigger plans and was keen to continue his running journey. He continued running, completing other events, and continued to progress. Twelve months after completing his first race he fronted up at the same event, this time keen to do even better. Unsurprisingly, given he had been committed to the process, he again achieved what he set out to do and had a fantastic race. John is now positioned to do this again for a third time. Steady, consistent run improvement over three years. John had learned to be patient and play the long game.

What we must realise here, of course, is that what John was able to achieve after three years was very different from what he was able to achieve in the first year I coached him. Had he tried to complete his third year training plan in his first year of running, it would have broken him. And we know that you can't win if you're broken. John continues to train with confidence and improve his running. He enjoys the journey and finishes with a smile. John is a Run Fit runner.

So now that I've warned you not to fall into the common runner's trap of short-term thinking, and convinced you that patience is necessary and that this is a long-tail game, let's look at the three parts of the Game Plan: strategy, deliberate practice, and a training and racing plan.

## STRATEGY

Strategy is the big picture. It's the long-term view I've just been talking about. Strategy is how you will get from point A to point B. Taking into account the key concepts we have covered above, we need to put in place a long-term strategy that is going to keep you motivated, progress you towards meaningful running goals and allow you to succeed.

This strategy needs to look at not just one race but a sequence of races, a progression, to allow your knowledge, skills, experience and fitness to build. By regularly and systematically extending your comfort zone just a little, we can choose a logical progression to achieve your desired goal or outcome. The strategy must take into account what you detailed earlier that you would like to achieve in twelve months, three years from now and over your lifetime. The other key to a good long-term strategy is to train holistically.

### The right races in the right order

When designing a strategy, it's important to choose a logical progression towards your goal. In terms of race sequencing, someone newer to running might choose to complete a series of 5 km events before progressing to a 10 km event and then a half marathon. Someone wanting to tackle a marathon for the first time might choose to complete a 10 km event, then a few half marathons before tackling their first marathon.  And a marathon runner looking to move up to completing their first 100 km event might decide to target a few 50 km ultras before moving up to their first 100 km ultra.

Unfortunately, what often happens is that runners decide they want to jump straight into training for the half marathon before they've even started doing any running at all. Or someone who has been tackling a few 5 km events suddenly wants to jump up to the marathon without completing some half marathons along the way. And the marathon runner wants to tackle the 100 km event without first targeting the 50 km ultra.

When this happens, runners take on far greater risks than they may appreciate. They risk injuries as they increase their run load too quickly. And then there's the mental side of things, which may not be obvious from the outside. These impatient runners regularly find themselves in a state of overwhelm and feel increased pressure to perform. They may be under-prepared and lack certainty on the start line because DNFs and race blow outs are very much a possibility. But they may have many of their supporters at the race, or cheering them on from home, and they don't want to let those supporters down. This pressure saps these runners' energy, enjoyment and the overall experience they have at the race.

But by avoiding the temptation of over-ambitious goals and instead choosing a logical progression of races, runners take the pressure off themselves. They enjoy their running more, because they can feel their comfort zone being challenged without being put into a state of overwhelm. Choosing a long-term, logical progression of races means that runners give their bodies time to adapt and time to learn and develop as a runner. All in all, they enjoy the experience and the journey more and finish with a smile. They are Run Fit runners.

### Strengths versus limiting factors

Your strategy for improvement needs to look beyond a sequence of races – race selection is simply the first step. We also need to look at what your strengths are and where your limiting factors are. Strengths are, obviously, what you do well. Limiting factors are what is limiting you in achieving your goals. I am a believer in a well-rounded or holistic running program that trains both strengths and limiting factors, but many runners neglect their limiting factors.

Marathon runners are a prime example of failing to create a well-rounded, holistic training program. Most think that it is going to be their fitness, specifically their aerobic fitness, that determines the outcome of their race. Few ever consider that it will be their running strength that will determine the outcome. As a result, both first time and even some experienced marathon runners might focus all their training on their fitness. My favourite question to ask at the end of a race is, 'What went first, your legs or the engine?' Before reading on, what is *your* answer? You may have guessed that for many it is in fact their legs. They start cramping before they reach the finish, and they're forced to undertake the dreaded soldier march to the finish line.

If we know that run strength is likely to be a particular runner's limiting factor, we can build a training plan that addresses this. If run strength let them down in their last race, we can undertake training that looks to prevent this in their next race. By identifying your limiting factors, either going into a race or post-race, you can develop a training plan that focuses your attention on these areas, corrects them, and thus allows you to reach your full human potential and have your personal best performance.

But there is another side to this. Simply because someone has a strength does not mean we should not train it. Yes, you read that right, I do not think we should spend all our time on improving our limiting factors. While I prefer to focus attention on developing your limiting factors, it is important to include *all* elements within the run program. After all, if you love doing something because you're good at it, we want to keep it in there and let you enjoy doing it. Once we have established your limiting factors, we need to ensure these are improved within your training program and that you understand how to develop them, but we also need to give you time to enjoy your strengths.

## DELIBERATE PRACTICE

This book's subtitle is 'Improve your running, finish with a smile'. So it would be remiss of me not to cover how to improve your running. While this whole book is about improving your running, it hinges on a key concept called deliberate practice. Deliberate practice is how anyone gets better at anything, yet it is often misunderstood. And because it is often misunderstood, it is regularly overlooked by coaches, who fail to properly implement it into training programs. In fact, most coaches choose to focus solely on improving their clients' fitness and ignore deliberate practice altogether. Many even miss other elements discussed in the Run Fit Method. This is a mistake, as they are leaving so much potential on the table. Often training plans simply consist of mileage charts (or kilometre charts). These charts are a pathetic excuse for a training plan, as they don't challenge or develop other aspects of the runner. So exactly what is deliberate practice, and why is it essential for you to undertake?

Deliberate practice is focused practice aimed at improving performance with a structure in place to help you get there. Anders Ericsson is the guru in this area. He summarised it as: 'Get outside your comfort zone but do it in a focused way, with clear goals, a plan for reaching those goals, and a way to monitor your progress. Oh and figure out a way to maintain your motivation.'[2]

Deliberate practice puts in place training techniques developed by others who have already figured out how to achieve a particular result. Goals are established, then broken down into smaller milestones

2 *Peak: How all of us can achieve extraordinary things*, Anders Ericsson and Robert Pool

to achieve along the way. By achieving these milestones, we improve our overall performance. The individual builds and modifies skills by focusing on particular aspects of those skills. This often requires building mental representations of what skilful performance looks, sounds and feels like.

Further, deliberate practice is exactly that, deliberate. It must use the attention of the individual to complete it. It must also involve feedback and modification of effort in response to that feedback. Initially this feedback will come from a teacher or coach. Then as the individual understands this feedback and gains experience, they can begin to monitor their own performance. All of this occurs gradually, and this step-by-step improvement eventually improves overall performance.

Another key element of deliberate practice is the need to extend an individual beyond their comfort zone. That is, they must train on the limit of what they can achieve. This cusp is where the improvement occurs.[3]

To help illustrate the point, let's look at what deliberate practice is *not*. If you're a basketballer, going down to the park to play some social basketball is not deliberate practice. If you're a golfer, playing your weekly round with your mates is not deliberate practice. If you're a runner, simply going out for a run is not deliberate practice.

Deliberate practice is practice that is intentional in its nature and designed to help you improve. The basketballer undertakes deliberate practice when they take twenty three-point shots from the same place

3 *Peak: How all of us can achieve extraordinary things*, Anders Ericsson and Robert Pool

in the court. They are repeating the same skill from the same location and getting immediate feedback on how they did (the basketball either went into the hoop or it didn't). The golfer similarly undertakes deliberate practice when they head out to their local course and rather than just playing a round of golf, they hit twenty balls from the same spot on the fairway and try to get each one onto the green, or ideally into the hole. The golfer is not playing a round or even a complete hole. They are repeating a skill and receiving immediate feedback – did the ball land on the green or not – then playing their next shot with this feedback in mind and the intention of getting better.

The above two examples are far from what I would consider enjoyable, but they are a good way to help you understand the key elements required in deliberate practice. They also help you further understand that slow and steady wins the race – this type of focused, deliberate training takes time and can't be rushed. Let's now transfer our knowledge to running. Fortunately, deliberate practice in running is something that I find not only enjoyable but thrive on. When you understand what it entails, I suspect you will too.

When we run, deliberate practice can take many forms. You can aim to get the same splits over run intervals (segments of running). You can try to keep your race pace consistent by completing two or three laps of 2–5 km over an undulating course. Or you can look to improve your nutrition and hydration by practising your planned race nutrition within segments of a long run.

The types of deliberate practice you can insert into your running are endless. However, many runners don't do any deliberate practice, yet still hope they will improve. They are, in essence, doing the equivalent of a social round of golf or social game of basketball every time they go running. Sure, it's fun, but you'll enjoy your running more if you build deliberate practice into it. Deliberate practice adds variety to your running. It makes it more challenging and increases the fun, and has the added benefit of allowing you to improve. Deliberate practice is essential for you to improve as a runner.

## TRAINING AND RACING PLANS

A training plan is exactly what it sounds like – an outline of all the runs you need to undertake over a week, a month and multiple months leading into your goal race or event. This is the backbone of improvement. This is what gives you the structure you need over these periods. It is also what gives you the structure you need over each and every run, as it outlines in detail exactly what you need to do.

It's the detail that's important and what makes a good training plan, but unfortunately many coaches put out run plans that are simply mileage charts or tables of distances. They contain no or very limited detail and also fail to include and embed deliberate practice. Mileage charts, as I like to call them because they are not a training plan, are simply designed to get you to run more. They are not focused on challenging you and allowing you to fast-track your improvement by improving your running skills, knowledge or experience. This is because they don't incorporate the deliberate practice we discussed above. Deliberate practice needs to be built into the training plan.

On the following page is an example of a mileage chart – it is not a training plan.

| Week | M | T | W | T | F | S | S | Total |
|---|---|---|---|---|---|---|---|---|
| 1 | Rest | 5 km | 5 km | 5 km | Rest | Cross-train | 10 km | 25 km |
| 2 | Rest | 6 km | 5 km | 6 km | Rest | Cross-train | 12 km | 29 km |
| 3 | Rest | 7 km | 5 km | 7 km | Rest | Cross-train | 15 km | 34 km |
| 4 | Rest | 8 km | 5 km | 8 km | Rest | Cross-train | 20 km | 41 km |
| 5 | Rest | 5 km | 7 km | 5 km | Rest | Cross-train | 16 km | 33 km |
| 6 | Rest | 9 km | 7 km | 9 km | Rest | Cross-train | 24 km | 49 km |
| 7 | Rest | 10 km | 7 km | 10 km | Rest | Cross-train | 30 km | 57 km |
| 8 | Rest | 10 km | 7 km | 10 km | Rest | Cross-train | 21 km | 48 km |
| 9 | Rest | 12 km | 9 km | 10 km | Rest | Cross-train | 32 km | 63 km |
| 10 | Rest | 12 km | 10 km | 7 km | Rest | Cross-train | 36 km | 65 km |
| 11 | Rest | 8 km | 7 km | 8 km | Rest | Cross-train | 16 km | 39 km |
| 12 | Rest | 7 km | 5 km | 3 km | Rest | Rest | 42.2 km | 57.2 km |

The training plan, as opposed to a mileage chart, is a detailed plan that outlines all your training sessions between where you are at the start of your training and where you want to be at the end of it. It guides you, gives you clarity, and allows you to achieve long-term, gradual progression. It brings in your strategy for improvement, outlining the sets you need to complete to overcome your limiting factors. It is a detailed training plan, meaning that it incorporates all the ideas and concepts we have discussed so far and also includes all the ideas and concepts we are yet to cover. In particular, it includes deliberate practice in the training sets. It is how we implement Run Fit. It allows you to improve your running and finish with a smile.

The training plan also has a layer built into it that may not be immediately apparent. This is periodization. Periodization is the sequential, systematic and structured approach to your training program that we touched on in Chapter 2. It takes into account weekly, monthly and multiple-month blocks leading into your race or chosen event, and will include times when you are building and recovering as well as a taper prior to the race. It allows gradual, controlled, consistent progression. If you follow the process, you will progress. If we improve our training, we improve our racing. Long-term, gradual progression leads to success.

Within the training plans that we write, we also like to include days that are designed to keep the adventure, fun and challenge in what you're doing. Being able to keep a runner engaged in the training program for a long period is vital to its success. To help with this we include things like Adventure Days, Run Explorer Days and Race Simulation Days, balancing these off with run sets that contain deliberate practice as well as a nice shot of running purely for the love of it. The aim is to strike the right balance that creates engagement without overwhelm.

### Tailoring

The plan must also be tailored to the runner, whether they're a new runner, a beginner, intermediate, advanced or elite. What can be achieved by an advanced or elite runner is, obviously, far in excess of what can be achieved by a new or beginner runner.

We use the following definitions to help provide clarity:

**New runner** – someone who has just started running

**New to formal run training** – someone who has been running for a while but is new to training that is structured in its nature and includes periodization

**Beginner** – 1–2 years of structured run training

**Intermediate** – 3–4 years of structured run training

**Advanced** – 5–6 years of structured run training

**Elite** – 7+ years of structured run training

The plan must also be specific for the runner's goal event. The types of training sets that a 5 km and 10 km runner should do are vastly different from the training sets that a marathon or ultra runner needs to do.

### Delivery

The training plan can be delivered in different ways. You can use a Word or Excel document, or online coaching software like Training Peaks, Today's Plan, Final Surge or 2Peak.

In our experience, a Word or Excel file is limited in the detail it can provide. It is simply too challenging for a coach to include all the required detail in a Word document or Excel spreadsheet. This is where online coaching software has an advantage due to the way information is contained within it.

Online software also has the advantage of allowing you or a coach to track, measure and review your training, and can therefore easily give you greater insight into what is occurring. It lets a coach see inside what you're doing. They are able to look at your training to review training sets and provide feedback on how you went, which helps implement the deliberate practice. This is something that simply cannot happen via a Word or Excel document. These insights can be gleaned from an individual set or year on year of training. By comparing sets over time or looking at your training year on year, you gain long-term insights and see trends that can give you confidence in your progress or highlight areas of concern.

### YOUR JOURNEY

You now know what a training plan is *not*. Head online to www.therunjourney.com and click on the Run Fit Club to find out what a true training plan should look like. Use the code RunFit to unlock your two-week free membership to the platform and your detailed training plan.

### ON THE RUN

Ask your run partner to head to The Run Journey as well so that you can both have a detailed training plan to follow and discuss while you run. This can even be beneficial when you don't run together, as you can complete the same sets independently and discuss your experience later.

## A race plan - the finishing touch

A detailed training plan is essential preparation for a great race. But don't fall at the last hurdle by failing to create a great race plan for your upcoming event. Runners regularly put hours upon hours into training for an event and then overlook this final step. They rock up on the start line expecting that things will just happen. A race plan is essential, because a great race doesn't just happen. It takes planning.

A race plan is needed so that you have confidence in what you are going to do when the gun goes off. Are you going to be charging off the line or are you going to be holding back and running your race properly? How are you going to fuel yourself over the run? What about hydration; how's that going to pan out? How will you pace yourself over the event? Where should you start? For the ultra races, what do you need to carry? These are questions that will make or break your race. You may have nailed your training plan and be exceptionally fit on the start line, but muck up one of these and you could be left walking to the finish line.

The reason we need a race plan is because, in the heat of the moment when the gun goes, you are going to get the biggest shot of adrenaline you have had in months. This, coupled with the fact that you're feeling great after a taper and recovery period and are emotionally invested in the outcome, is a recipe for disaster. Why? Because runners in that state regularly overestimate what they're capable of. They start off well, thinking, 'I'm not only going to blitz this race, I'm going to annihilate my PB.' Then suddenly things change, and their race starts falling apart as fatigue creeps in and their ambitions are destroyed.

On the other hand, the runner who goes in with a solid race plan has thought about what they are going to do while they are cool, calm and unemotional. In this state they can make calculated and educated decisions based on what they have achieved in training. With this plan in place they have a starting point for dealing with problems during the event. They know what plan 'A' is and they can adjust this as necessary or as challenges arise.

Naturally a 10 km or half marathon plan will be very different from an ultramarathon plan in its detail. Nevertheless, thought has to be put into how the race will unfold *before* the runner is on the start line.

## CONCLUSION

Phew – we have just covered a mammoth amount of information. But, as I said, the Game Plan is the backbone of Run Fit. You are now aware that you must lose the bias towards short-term thinking that many runners have and transition into a new understanding that long-term, gradual progression leads to success. You know that the Game Plan is what allows us to achieve this.

The Game Plan consists of three main parts. You have learned that strategy for improvement includes developing a sequence of races and identifying your limiting factors and strengths. Together these allow us to take a holistic approach to your running. You now also understand what deliberate practice is, and if you want to improve it must be implemented through the run training plan. Finally you understand the need for a detailed training plan and racing plan. You have seen that a mileage chart is not a training plan and have jumped online and started your free two-week training plan, which shows what a detailed training plan actually looks like. Hopefully you have started to feel the success that it can bring you as a runner.

At this point your understanding around Run Fit is progressing beautifully. Stick with it as we move on to developing your mindset.

CHAPTER 4

# MINDSET

*All improvement must happen in the mind before it can happen in the body*

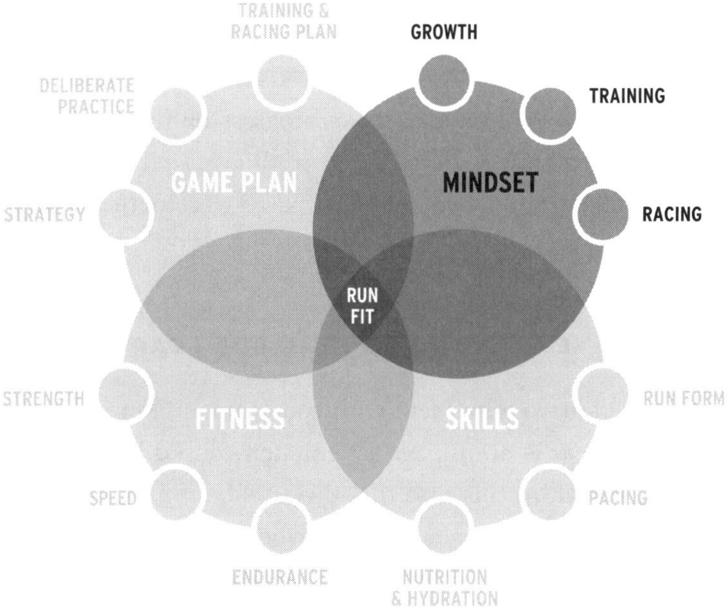


To be a good runner you need a good mindset. To be a great runner you need a great mindset. All improvement must happen in the mind before it can happen in the body. This means we must look to develop your mindset during your training program, or even before you begin training. If you don't first think that you can do something, you are not even going to get started. As a runner you are going to break your mindset into the following three key areas and work on developing each one:

- growth mindset,
- training mindset; and
- racing mindset.

Before we look in depth at each of these areas, we're going to unpack an important concept: fear and why it can hold you back from realising your dreams. This concept needs to be understood to ensure we start and continue to make progress on the run training plan. Without a clear understanding of this you will remain idle – wanting to start but never being prepared to actually commit to reaching your audacious goals.

## YOU HAVE NOTHING TO FEAR BUT FEAR ITSELF

Most runners have a problem with commitment. More precisely, they fear it. Fear is an unpleasant emotion caused by a threat or perceived threat. In this case that threat is failure. Runners have a problem with commitment because when you commit to a goal, you also create the possibility of failure. The more audacious the goal, the bigger the possibility of failure. And it's failure that most runners are really afraid of.

If you jump in and commit to something, then you have no excuse. You have to own the outcome – both what happens in your training and in the event you are training for. That's a lot of commitment to take on. It's easier to do nothing… when you don't try, you can't fail.

If you don't commit you always have an excuse as to why you failed, and there are many. I don't have the time. I work too much. I'm not very good at running uphill. I'm not fit enough; I struggle over the back part of the race. I always goof up my nutrition. I don't have the strength. I never get the training right.

But you have a choice. Continue to follow the same path or face your fears, make a change and commit. The choice is yours as to what you do with your life and where you spend your time.

What is the story you're telling yourself? Does it feature any of the excuses listed above? Become aware of that story and, if need be, change it. Listen to the excuses you make. Is there a better story you can tell yourself? For instance...

**Excuse:** I can't get the training done because I don't have time.

**Alternative story:** I will fit in the training that I can and do the best with my given circumstances.

**Excuse:** I work too much.

**Alternative story:** I will prioritise my health and wellbeing to fit in the running that I can.

**Excuse:** I am not very good at running uphill.

**Alternate story:** I will practise running uphill in training.

**Excuse:** I am not very good at my nutrition.

**Alternative story:** I will practice my nutrition in training till I get it right.

**Excuse:** I am not fit enough.

**Alternative story:** I will develop my fitness in training.

Like I said, it's not really commitment you're afraid of. It's failure that you're afraid of, and fear is clouding your judgement. Like Churchill said, 'You have nothing to fear but fear itself.' In fact, commitment is the antidote to your fear. Commit and you will succeed. Yes, it's a lot of commitment to take on to personally own the outcome. But if you put in place the steps outlined in this book, you will succeed. And when you do succeed? Then dream a bigger dream and go again.

Now that I have convinced you not to be afraid and to commit to your audacious running goal, we need to look at the three key areas of mindset crucial to being Run Fit. It all starts with building our growth mindset as a runner.

## GROWTH MINDSET

The story you tell yourself is nicely explained by Dr Carol Dweck in her book *Mindset*. Your mindset will be somewhere on a spectrum from fixed to growth.

At one end of the spectrum is the fixed mindset – someone at this point on the spectrum believes they can't change in a fundamental way. You are either good or you are not. You are either good at running hills or you are not. You are either good at nailing your nutrition or you are not. You either have the time to fit training in or you don't. When we have this mindset, we blame others and create excuses when things go wrong. But this is just our mind's way of coping with a belief that we're not good enough. Our mind is being driven by fear. When we are in this state our ego is being attacked, and we will do anything and everything to keep our ego intact.

At the other end of the spectrum is the growth mindset. This is a fully empowering mindset. If you have this mindset you thrive on the work because you know that your commitment to the process is what delivers results. You tell yourself a very different story. That no one was ever great at anything the first time; they must have worked hard to be able to achieve what they did. So you say to yourself, 'I can work hard; I will achieve the same results.'

It is important to note that you may have a fixed mindset for certain aspects of your life and a growth mindset for others. You could have a fixed mindset when it comes to running, but a growth mindset when it comes to learning a language. You may have a growth mindset when it comes to running, but a fixed mindset when it comes to playing an instrument. You may even have a fixed mindset on some aspects of your running and a growth mindset for other aspects. For example, you could believe you have great running speed but really suck at managing hydration.

We need to develop and shift our thinking to a growth mindset with everything that we do. We need to focus on the process, not the outcome. If we focus on the process of getting better rather than attaching ourselves to the outcome, then we put ourselves into a position to improve regardless of what the final outcome is.

Such an approach allows us to remove our ego from how our training goes and how our race goes. We stop judging ourselves. With this ego removed we are free to commit to the best of our ability and enjoy the process of improvement. If we focus our attention in this way, the outcomes will eventually take care of themselves.

Developing a growth mindset allows you to have a positive attitude in your training and your racing. A Run Fit runner has developed a growth mindset with respect to all aspects of their run training and racing. It allows you to foster a strong belief in yourself and your abilities.

### Accept change

Another reason that it's important to have a growth mindset is that it allows you to accept change. And you must change if you want to fulfil your full potential as a runner. The runner with a growth mindset accepts change. To change is to grow. But if to change is to grow, why are so many people fearful of change? They are fearful of change because it is different.

Doing something differently always feels weird, awkward and uncomfortable at the start. It's easier to continue the way you were. But to stay that way is to not reach your full human potential. To not achieve all the dreams and goals that you set out in Chapter 1. We need to accept that making a change does feel weird, awkward and uncomfortable at the start and go through with it anyway. A Run Fit runner embraces this change, commits to the process and knows they will improve and enjoy the journey of achieving their running goals.

## TRAINING MINDSET

Now that I've explained that you have to be in the right mental space to grow and change, let's look at your training mindset. To develop our training mindset, we need to ensure we foster our self-belief, focus on what matters and spend time reflecting.

To improve your running, we need to develop and foster your self-belief. The mind needs to know that the body is capable; that you are capable. If the mind knows these things, we can fast-track your running.

Self-belief is built through the training plan. The training plan is how we build your confidence in what you are capable of. It does this because it allows you to become an *experienced* runner. In all aspects of your running, we gradually get you closer and closer to what you will experience in your event. This means that when you front up at the start line you have very clear and proven knowledge of your capabilities. You have been there before. For example, we can build up the experience you have with pacing by challenging you more and more with the run sets that develop this skill. When it comes to your race, you will have a solid amount of experience with pacing.

We can also use visualisation to help you feel like you have 'been there before'. Visualisation is imagining yourself performing in your mind's eye. You can see yourself having a great race and finishing strong. You can see yourself having a race where nothing goes to plan, but where you overcome each and every challenge that tries to hold you back and run smiling to the finish line. Visualisation works because while your body has not actually completed the event or the activities that you have visualised, your mind thinks you have. This means that if and when problems that you have rehearsed mentally crop up in reality, you feel as though you have been there before and will know what to do.

The training plan will also help you get comfortable being uncomfortable. When you can tolerate discomfort, you know you can get through the difficult moments and this in turn boosts your self-belief. Remember that being uncomfortable means that you are growing – edging your fitness, knowledge, experience and mindset further. The discomfort that occurs at this time is fleeting compared to the success that you will have on race day. Get used to it. This is you building your self-belief.

But remember that believing in yourself doesn't mean being too proud to get help. Quite the contrary. We each have different areas where we excel and areas where we are developing. Just as you would be able to help a novice in your area of expertise, seek guidance from others. Those who have achieved what you wish to achieve, those who have previously completed the races you wish to complete, and those who have experience beyond what you have. Help could come from individuals you know, through joining run clubs and groups, or from seeking the assistance of a running coach such as me.

### Focus on what matters

To improve your running, you are going to have to put mental focus into what you're doing. This is where the rubber hits the road on the deliberate practice. You may be focusing on your pacing, focusing on your run form, focusing on your ability to maintain a positive mindset.

You also need to focus on what is in your control. Not everything will go perfectly in training, and it certainly won't all go perfectly when you race. You need to be able to adapt, overcome unplanned challenges and continue. A work meeting could come up that clashes with your training schedule. How will you manage to fit your training set in? Can you prioritise your running and the long-term enjoyment it will bring over the short-term enjoyment of watching TV and using social media? By controlling what you can, you empower yourself to make decisions that help you achieve your running dreams. This is how mental toughness is developed; through making the hard decisions in training, through being positive and proactive in the face of adversity.

### Reflect and learn

Reflection can also help you fast-track your success. How often do we catch ourselves saying, 'If only I had known?' Hindsight can be invaluable; however, people are often disappointed that they don't get to act on the insights they have after an event. But you are a runner, and you will face the same circumstances again. You will get another chance to improve.

That is one of the goals of the training plan. To set up teaching experiences so that you can develop and implement lessons learned when you face the same situation again – in the training program and then ultimately in your race. The ability to do this revolves around reflecting on how you are going and where you would like to improve.

I love the Japanese word Kaizen. It means continuous change and improvement for the better. If we embody the meaning of this word with our running, we will never stop training, never stop learning and never stop growing. Take the time to reflect on both your training and your racing. Valuable lessons always present themselves, which you can take into subsequent training sessions or races.

When you reflect you will often identify areas where you went wrong, but it is also essential that you celebrate the small victories.

Runners, being driven people, are always chasing the next big race and next big PB. Once those goals are achieved, they're straight away chasing the next one. You need to celebrate the small victories. You had a really good run and achieved your focus, so celebrate it and acknowledge what you achieved. If you completed every run set for the week, celebrate that success. If you completed the strength or stretching set that you often miss, celebrate your success. Celebrating these small successes along the way will have a massive effect on building your momentum. When you celebrate these small victories, you enhance the dopamine effect in your brain. This is using dopamine in its original, intended way as opposed to the kick you get out of getting a few likes on a social media post. Celebrate the meaningful victories and build your momentum for success.

## RACING MINDSET

Now we come to your racing mindset. Here we will cover three key areas – noise, flow and positivity. By ensuring you have a good strong racing mindset, you put yourself in the best possible place to have success on event day. You will be calm on the start line and smiling at the finish line.

### Ignore the noise

Your race begins, obviously, on the start line. But even before this moment you need to lock in your racing mindset. The first challenge will be noise. The noise leading into your event is normally deafening. It's everywhere. But it's not the noise from shouting and screaming that I'm talking about. It's the noise from other people in the days and weeks before. Others who doubt their own abilities. They will talk to you, question your training. How many speed sets have you done? How many long runs have you completed? How many marathon pace sets have you done? What's your longest run? They're questioning you because they are questioning themselves and their own preparation. If they get you to doubt yourself as well, then that makes them feel better. Don't listen. Trust in your training, trust in the process that you have followed, believe in yourself. Sure, listen to what they have to say if you wish to be polite, but don't take on their ideas. If you have followed a quality and detailed training plan, you are ready. You will know from what you have achieved in training that you are ready. In running, preparation never lies.

### Find flow

You are now on the start line. You are prepared. You have the knowledge and the skills. You have undertaken the practice. You are fit. It now comes down to race day execution. The final noise you will hear on the start line is the starter's gun. Then you're off and racing. Now the key in your racing mindset is to find that all-important state of flow.

Flow is the ability to be fully immersed in the present moment. Runners regularly report a simultaneous speeding up and slowing down of time when they enter such a state. When you're in a state of flow, you are not worried about the things on your to-do list like doing the washing, walking the dog, taking the kids to sports practice. Nor are you worried about the future. You're not thinking about going on a holiday to Hawaii one day or that you would like to buy a house in a few years. You're not worried about the past, either. You don't waste time wishing you could change a decision you made at work, or indeed in your training. You are here and now. Such a state allows intense focus and concentration. You will perform at your best when you enter a state of flow. Understanding this and looking to regularly enter a state of flow – in your training and especially when racing – will ensure you love your journey from the start line to the finish line.

### Stay positive

To have a great race you need to be cool, calm and collected. You need to be relaxed but alert. Ready to go. Your belief in yourself has been built through the training plan, and you will need to stay positive through to the end. While this may sound easy on paper, to achieve this in a race is often much more challenging. You need to develop the ability to stay in a positive frame of mind. And if a negative mindset begins to creep in, you need to learn how to snap it back to positivity.

The easiest way to do this is to be in control of your thoughts and your body language. Recognise if you are having negative thoughts about how you currently feel in the race. If this occurs, change those thoughts to positive ones. Change 'I'm starting to feel fatigued, I don't think I can do this,' to 'I am a strong runner; I am running strong.' If this doesn't get the job done, then look at your body language and ensure this is positive. If you're slumped in your running, shift your body language to being positive. Engaged through the core, running tall and strong. If you're frowning, smile. Repeat the process till you have won the battle and are again running well and feeling positive.

You can also use positive self-talk and mantras, which you should develop and practise in training. Mantras can help you run well over the final part of a race or up hills, or sail effortlessly through aid stations. I have three mantras. Throughout the race, to make sure all is on track, I say, 'Nutrition, hydration, pacing, patience, positivity.' To ensure I have great run form at the end of a race I repeat to myself, 'Run tall and drive the knees.' To ensure I run well through check points, I mentally rehearse my actions on the way in and repeat, 'Smooth is fast.' Feel free to use these or come up with your own that work for you.

Finally, play to win – your win. You deserve this, so rise to the occasion and shine. You are a Run Fit runner. Get out there, show your stuff and achieve all you ever hoped to achieve. And don't forget to finish with a smile.

## CONCLUSION

You now have the knowledge to build the mindset of a champion. You are able to overcome your fear of failure and understand that commitment to the process will give you the best chance of succeeding.

You are aware that there are three key principles that need to be developed in the runner: growth mindset, training mindset and racing mindset. You know that everyone has either a fixed or a growth mindset, and we must take action to ensure we have a growth mindset with all aspects of our running. You are also aware of the need for positive change and the fact that so many people shy away from this change because it is different, but not you – you embrace it. When looking at your training mindset, you know that you need to foster your self-belief, develop your focus and use your ability to reflect to learn from and correct past mistakes as you move forward. When racing, you know you need to harness your racing mindset and deploy tactics to ensure it stays in place. This includes ignoring the pre-race noise, utilising flow and maintaining a positive mindset while you race.

A Run Fit runner works to improve their mindset regularly and recognises this as a process. It takes time, fortitude and commitment to develop an impenetrable fortress of the mind. You are now primed to launch into developing your skills as a runner. Let's go.

CHAPTER 5

# SKILLS

*Follow the process to progress*

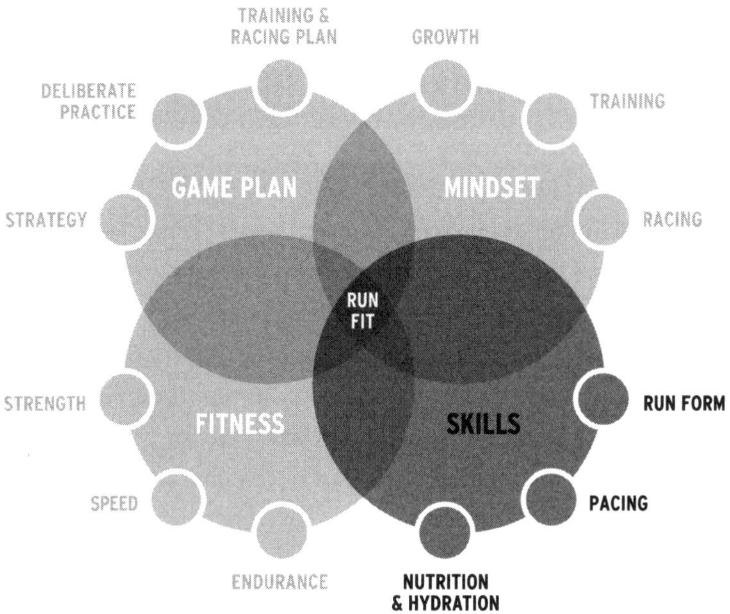


To be better runners, we have to have a sound understanding of how to run. Once we have this understanding of how to run, the specific mechanics, we then need to develop the skills required by the runner. Your skill set has three key components:

- run form,

- pacing; and
- nutrition and hydration.

Before we get to those three components, however, we have to lay the groundwork for understanding them by looking at a key concept that underpins your training – that everyone is different and that you are training for different events.

## IT'S HORSES FOR COURSES

When it comes to running skills, all runners need the same ones. However, the way those skills are deployed during a race depends on the nature of the event. And the training plan for that event needs to focus on and develop the right skills in the right way. This is why the Run Fit Method works. The skills are fundamental and unchanging – it's the way the method is implemented that changes. We need to be aware that from the 5 km through to the ultramarathon, the principles are implemented in a different manner. We need to be guided by the fundamental principles of our chosen event and also by our own personal preference.

For example, the run form used in a 5 km event, being fast and powerful, will look different from that used in an ultramarathon event, where you need to be economical and conservative in your running. Your body type and make-up may also affect the way you need to run in a particular event.

When it comes to pacing, be aware that the pacing applied by the elites in a 5 km event is different from what you should apply in your goal event. The elites race to win and there are often surges in their races as they look to drop competitors. Rarely do they go out to race the clock and attempt to set a PB. If you're only intent on beating the person next to you, then such tactics and strategies may come into play. The point is that you need to be clear on your goals with respect to your race so that you can implement your pacing correctly.

Nutrition and hydration are also uniquely individual. You cannot simply copy what your running partner does and expect it to work for you. Mistakes made with nutrition and hydration can lead to stomach upset, gastrointestinal distress and, in the extreme, diarrhoea. If you don't take adequate nutrition you can hit the wall, and if you become overly dehydrated you'll have a lacklustre performance and may have to walk to the finish line. But everyone's needs are different, so you need to take the guiding principles and apply them to yourself and your chosen event.

To sum up, what we need to do is look at how we can best implement the guiding principles to work for your unique body in your goal event.

## RUN FORM

The first element of your skill set as a runner is your run form. To be able to refine our run form we first have to understand the variables that make up our pace, or speed, while running. Our pace is made up of two variables that we can change to allow ourselves to run quicker. It is neatly expressed in the following formula.

**Pace = Cadence x Stride Length**

Based on this, we can see that to increase our pace we can do one of two things. We can increase our cadence – the number of strides we take per minute – which is determined by how often our legs hit the ground. Or we can increase our stride length. There is nothing more to it.

This means that to become a faster runner, we need to develop our ability to do one or both of the above. But how we go about achieving this has many paths. We can improve your fitness, which will be discussed in the next chapter, or we can look to improve your economy. We'll discuss economy shortly, but first let's take a look at cadence.

### Cadence

There are a few misconceptions that come up with cadence. Many people say that the best cadence is 90 strides per minute if you count the number of times one leg hits the ground over a minute, or 180 if you count both legs.

The shorter the running race we're in and the faster we wish to run, the higher our cadence is likely to be. Hence a runner who is running a 5 km race is likely to simultaneously increase both their stride length and cadence to allow their pace to increase. This means that they may run at a cadence in excess of 180 for the duration of the race. But place the same runner in a marathon and their cadence is likely to be lower than what they hold in their 5 km event, as they would be unable to hold a higher cadence for the time it takes to complete a marathon. It takes too much energy. This is a classic example of how different events, different runners and different situations require a different approach.

What typically happens when someone tries to increase their cadence is that they keep their stride length the same. Consequently, all they're doing is running faster – and that takes more energy. Runners often have a breakthrough if they can understand that to increase their cadence and keep their pace the same, they have to decrease their stride length. After all, it is the only other variable in the equation on page 91.

If runners are able to slightly decrease their stride length to allow their cadence to increase while holding the same pace, they often find they are more comfortable and economical in their running, and start to develop a greater sense that they're floating, or indeed running as you should run. This comes from the runner reducing ground impact forces, which has the added benefit of reducing the chance of injury for a win/win scenario. While I don't subscribe to the idea that your cadence has to be at or above 90, I do often encounter runners whose cadence is too low. I have found that runners seem to find running easier and improve their economy if their cadence is above 85 strides per minute.

When I discuss cadence with runners, I find that many have tried to improve their cadence before without success. To give them confidence that change can happen and that they can improve, I love to share the story of Anna. Her cadence was in the 65–75 range and she was trying to muscle her way through her runs. After discussing these concepts with her, we implemented some deliberate practice with regards to her cadence. Anna took this knowledge out on her runs and practised and practised, grappling with the challenge that was presented to her. Slowly but surely her cadence improved.

A cadence of 70 became a consistent 75, 75 became 77, 77 became 82 and she was almost there. Finally, she reached the 85–90 range. Anna now sits at a comfortable cadence in the 85–90 range and has steadily improved her running. Anna was able to unlock free speed by improving her cadence, and now Anna is a Run Fit runner.

### YOUR JOURNEY

When out on a run, count your cadence. Do this by either looking at the cadence displayed on your watch or by mentally counting your cadence. You can calculate your cadence by counting it for fifteen seconds and then multiplying this number by four. If you count the number of times one leg strikes the ground, you are aiming for a number between 85 and 90. If you count the times both legs strike the ground, you are aiming for a number between 170 and 180.

### ON THE RUN

Count your running partner's cadence when training. How does your cadence compare to theirs?

## Economy

Economy is the amount of oxygen needed to allow you to run at any given pace. If we can improve our running economy we can increase our running pace, as we have more oxygen available that we can use to propel us forwards instead of wasting it on unnecessary movement. The oxygen is going where it is needed, not where it isn't.

A runner's goal is to get from point A to point B in as short a time as possible. With this in mind, we run in a straight line between two points – you wouldn't take a detour along the way! This is an important concept that we need to understand with respect to our economy. Running is about using your legs to get your centre of mass as quickly as possible from point A to point B.

But what happens for many runners is that economy of movement breaks down. They start to incorporate force in a lateral plane, using left to right movement. Also, more often than not they include additional force in the vertical plane, moving their centre of gravity up and down. On a run watch you see this listed as vertical oscillation. For the runner to achieve these movements requires effort, or oxygen. If we are able to reduce the forces in each of these planes – both lateral and vertical – this effort can be put to better use to allow us to increase our forward momentum or pace.

Tied in with this is the ground reaction force, which is the force exerted through the leg during the contact phase of running. We want to minimise the ground reaction force. For many runners this is a large breaking force that slows their pace. You will see this listed on a run watch as ground contact time (GCT). If we are able to decrease this force, then we are better able to keep our momentum and reduce our injury risk. Thus, rather than having to generate all the energy for each and every stride, we are able to use the energy already generated in one stride in the next one. This therefore improves your running economy. When these things all come together, you have improved your running form and are more economical in your movement. And thus you are faster.

Elite runners are very economical in their movement. They have a great understanding of where their centre of gravity is, how they are holding their hips, how they are carrying their arms, and where their feet are making contact with the ground and how. They are able to hold their body position precisely where they want it to allow them the most economical movement. Together these factors mean that they have low vertical oscillation, low ground reaction forces and low ground contact time. They are highly economical runners.

As your run form improves, you are able to reduce unwanted forces and shift more of the energy you are creating to where you will benefit from it. This ultimately leads to improved economy and better run form. The best way to achieve this is through run drills and training sets curated with a focus on run form. You should incorporate sets like this as a part of your Game Plan, specifically building these into the training program over the year.

### ON THE RUN

1. When out running, analyse your running partner's form. What are they doing well? What do you think they need to improve? How does their running form compare to yours?
2. Make a video of each other running. Watch it back to analyse your run form. Do this together every 6–12 months and save the videos to track your improvement over time. The change of seasons can be a great prompt to do this. First week of summer, first week of winter.

### YOUR JOURNEY

1. Look to analyse other runners. You could do this when you're running or even when you're driving your car or out walking and see other people running.
2. Head to the internet and find videos of runners to analyse.

## PACING

The next skill that you need as a runner is pacing. Pacing is required in all running events from 5 km through to 100 miles. Pacing is not the same as pace. *Pace* is how fast you run – your speed – and we discussed that earlier in this chapter. *Pacing* is how you control that speed over the duration of a race. It is the ability to control your output over the period of time required to run the event, giving you the best outcome possible. You finish in the quickest time possible. The winner isn't the first to the 5 km mark (or, in a 5 km race, the 1 km mark), the winner is the first to the finish line. You must look to develop a pacing plan going into your race and practise this in training. And even though every race is different, the Run Fit Method provides a formula that can standardise your approach to pacing, regardless of the type of event you're running.

To understand why we need to pace ourselves, we need to understand how fatigue occurs in the body. To pace yourself is the best way, physiologically, to deliver your personal best result. Let me put this in simple terms. Because of the way the body functions, two things happen if you overshoot in your running. First, you push your energy systems too far. This means that they need to have a period of recovery before you can return to a sustainable level. You may have experienced this in training if you have run a hard interval, started too quickly over the first half and then struggled to the finish point. This type of pacing challenge occurs more often in shorter distance races, where runners can push their blood lactate levels too high early in a race.

Second, you 'damage' your muscles. This is actually what you do when training, and is what helps you build strength – when the muscles recover, they come back stronger. However, this recovery takes days, and in a race you don't have days for this to happen. Muscle damage equates to fatigue, so if you get your pacing wrong when racing, it equates to an exponential loss of time over the second half of your race.

To sum up, if you overshoot your energy systems, you need to back off to allow yourself to recover. If you overshoot for a prolonged period relative to your race distance, then you accumulate too much fatigue (muscle damage) early, and this causes you to slow exponentially over the remainder of the race.

You may have heard people talk about the famed negative split. This is when you run the second half of your race quicker than the first half. And it's not all that hard to achieve if you go in with a pacing plan as part of your race plan. If, however, you go in without a plan of action, then a negative split is exceedingly hard to achieve. Ironically, this is because you are going to feel fantastic on the start line. You will have had a taper (recovery period) leading into your event, and when that gun fires something special happens. You get a massive shot of adrenaline. This means that you will feel like you can run hard for days. It causes your perception of your pace and effort to be skewed. We need to understand this and account for it. Good pacing builds in a safeguard that allows you to have a great race every time, but also allows you the freedom to run faster and exceed your expectations when it counts.

Like everything else, pacing is practised through deliberate training sets as part of the Game Plan. The ability to pace yourself doesn't just happen; it takes focused practice. The added benefit of practising pacing in training is that training improves, and with improved training we fast-track our fitness gains (discussed in the next chapter). This is because suddenly you are not fading toward the end of your intensity efforts or unable to complete your long runs.

The classic story to illustrate the importance of pacing comes from Kyle Chalmers' gold medal swim in the 100 m freestyle at the 2016 Olympics in Rio. If pacing is required in the 100 m freestyle, an event that takes under fifty seconds to complete, then it becomes clear that pacing is required for every running event from the 5 km through to 100 miles. Kyle went through the 50 m mark in that race placed seventh in a field of eight. After his win, Kyle said in reference to the half-way point of the race that he knew 'once I came off that wall I had to build'. He even acknowledged that 'I faded towards the end there'. While he came out on top, he was worried that he didn't quite nail his pacing.[4] Kyle is an elite swimmer who practises day in and day out and is one of the best in the world. This really helps to illustrate pacing's importance for us as runners and how challenging it is to nail your pacing.

### YOUR JOURNEY

Go back to a race you have completed and look at your time. See how long it took you to complete the first half compared to the second half. Did you manage to hit a negative split? How much did you hit

4 https://www.youtube.com/watch?v=do2X3gx7Kic
Accessed 10 November 2020

a negative split by? Or how much did you miss it by? If you missed it by more than five per cent you have plenty of scope for improvement, which can be made through improving your pacing.

## NUTRITION AND HYDRATION

To be Run Fit you need to have a sound understanding around your nutrition and hydration and how they affect your running. There are two parts to this: in-race nutrition and hydration and out-of-race nutrition and hydration. You need to understand both to become a Run Fit runner.

Out-of-race, you need to make sure that your nutrition and hydration is adequate to allow your body to recover, adapt and grow stronger. We also need to make sure that it is adequate to allow you to complete your training well. This means ensuring you have a balanced diet including quality protein, fats, carbohydrate and fibre, and that you are eating an abundance of fresh fruit and vegetables. You also need to ensure that you are timing your nutritional intake to allow you to finish your training sets well and back up for your next run.

The in-race nutrition you need depends on the length of the race. For races between 90 and 120 minutes, you will normally have enough fuel and hydration on board to allow you to finish.[5] You may choose to have a drink of water, a gel or some electrolyte if it's on offer, but this is a personal preference. For races over 120 minutes, in-race nutrition and hydration become essential. You simply do not have enough energy (nutrition) or water (hydration) in your body to allow you

5 www.sportsdietitians.com.au

to run the event without replenishment. As the events get longer, the complexity of achieving this increases. For a half marathon, you may need to have a couple of gels and water along the way. For ultra events, you need to be consuming more foods or different types of foods, and may even need to consider having meals on the run.

Along with this you need to be on top of your hydration. A drop in hydration of as little as two per cent has been shown to affect performance. At five per cent dehydration becomes dangerous, so you need to prevent it.[6] This means that you are going to need to consume water or electrolyte during your event.

To stay on top of your hydration requires an understanding of your own personal sweat rates relative to the conditions you are running in. Like I said at the beginning of this chapter – it's horses for courses and you need to know what works for you and how to adapt to the prevailing conditions. And, you guessed it, just like everything else, we need to develop your knowledge through the training plan and include nutrition and hydration as part of your race plan. Even if you're exceptionally fit, if you fail on your nutrition or hydration in training or in a race you can fail to achieve your potential. Your body won't have the fuel or hydration needed to power you through to the end of your training set or event.

Like everything else, nutrition and hydration are practised through carefully constructed training sets as part of the Game Plan. The ability to understand how to fuel your body doesn't just happen; it takes focused practice. Like pacing, this in turn has the ability to

6 Suzanne Girard Eberle, MS, RDN, CSSD, *Endurance Sports Nutrition – fuel your body for optimal performance*, 3rd edn, Human Kinetics, 2014

improve your training sets. You finish them feeling stronger, and you will obtain better training adaptations from sets that you finish well.

I understand nutrition and hydration really well, but that has not prevented me from coming unstuck. I clearly remember competing in 5 Peaks – a 58 km ultra run in South Australia. I had run well the whole day, but before I went through the final aid station I had a brain fade. While racing I deviated from my plan and misjudged how far I had to go to the finish line, so I didn't take enough fuel with me when I went through the station. When I realised the mistake I was too far out of the aid station to go back, yet still had 8 km to go. I felt my pace drop as my body started to struggle. I knew what was happening, but I had no way of preventing it. I had to accept the outcome and continue through to the finish line as best I could. I remember running sections with my eyes closed as I tried to embrace the mental effort needed before pulling myself together and attempting to look strong as I crossed the finish line.

The key take-away here is that you need a sound understanding of how to fuel and hydrate your body, and this needs to be practised and refined in training and then built into your race plan.

## YOUR JOURNEY

How will you change and improve your nutrition and hydration in your next race?

**1.**

**2.**

**3.**

If you are unsure, head online to www.therunjourney.com and join the Run Fit Club, where you will find a Nutrition and Hydration course. Use the code RunFit to unlock your two-week free membership to the platform, which will give you access to the course.

## CONCLUSION

You now understand the skill set of the runner and appreciate that this must be developed through deliberate practice built into the Game Plan. You must be able to apply the principles to yourself and your unique body, preferences and choice of race.

Within the skill set of Run Fit, you know that there are three areas that you must improve to help you succeed. Firstly, your run form. You have an appreciation for the two variables you can improve to increase your pace – cadence and stride length. You are aware that these can be developed through improvements in your running economy. You are also aware of the links between running economy and cadence and the need to boost your cadence if it is low. Secondly, you are aware of the need to improve your pacing, and you understand that it must be practised in your training plan. The same applies to the third skill that you must develop – nutrition and hydration. All these skills must be developed as part of your training program and implemented appropriately in your chosen race distance.

With the fundamental skills of the runner now covered, we are in a position to move to the chapter you have been long waiting for. Fitness. Let's roll.

CHAPTER 6

# FITNESS

*You can't fake fitness*

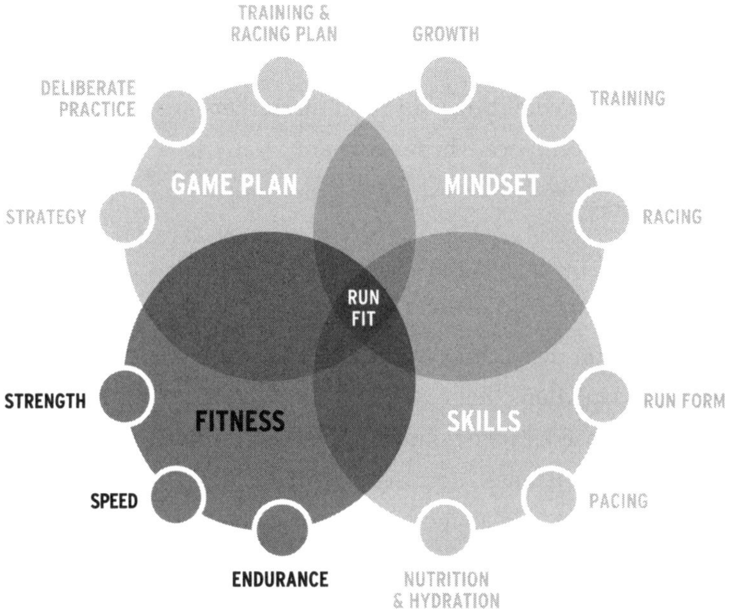


Fitness is having the physical condition to perform the task you wish to undertake. Here we are concerned with the ability to perform the task of running at the pace you wish for the duration of time you wish to perform it. Naturally we always wish to decrease the duration of this time over any distance. Thus, every runner always wants to build their run fitness. But as you are now aware, fitness is only one part of the equation when it comes to being Run Fit.

Your run fitness depends on having all of the other components of Run Fit in place. This is because improving the other elements allows you to improve your run *pace* without needing to improve your run *fitness*. Then, when we improve your run fitness and add that to the mix, you get a double whammy – an exponential net win! I can see that smile as the realisation of this vital concept becomes clear. In essence, the other elements are giving you free speed – an increase in pace that does not require building your fitness.

When it comes to building your run fitness, there are three areas that will improve your pace. Those areas are:

- endurance,
- speed; and
- strength.

By focusing on these three areas we can ensure we achieve all the fabulous adaptations that come from improving your fitness. These include increased stroke volume, increased muscle capilliarisation, increased red cell mass, increased plasma volume, increased muscle fibre recruitment, and an increase in the size of muscle fibres.

With the Game Plan in place, we can build out all three areas systematically. If the Game Plan is not in place, your training plan may take a scattered approach. Runners attempting to build their fitness without a game plan typically focus all their effort in one area, for instance endurance, only to overlook speed or strength – or both. Another common mistake is to only focus on speed while not building your endurance or strength. Also, runners often focus on an area of run fitness, endurance, speed or strength at the wrong time with respect to their goal race.

All three areas must be trained to build your run fitness. If you miss one you will leave time on the table and fail to achieve your full potential. You will fall short of your goal of being Run Fit. But before we look at each of these in detail, we first have to understand a critical concept: there is no magic set that on its own will make you Run Fit.

## THERE IS NO MAGIC BULLET

You may have heard people talk about the 'magic bullet' or the 'silver bullet' when they're looking for a quick, painless, guaranteed solution to a thorny problem. Of course, there usually is no such solution. And it's the same with running. There is no 'magic set' that, when practised, will guarantee you cross the finish line of your chosen event with a smile. Instead, what you need to do is put your body into a state of quality training repetitively. If you do this, it will adapt. This is how you build your fitness. So let's unpack what is meant by 'quality training' and 'repetitively'.

Quality training revolves around the understanding that the body adapts differently at different training intensities. Different intensities place different physiological demands on the body, and by changing this we can develop different components of your run fitness. Runners understand this best when it is put in the following way...

Everybody in any race from the last finisher to the first finisher has different paces they can run at, from a very slow warm-up and warm-down pace to an all-out sprint. Within this range we have a further range of paces or intensities. For instance your ultramarathon pace, your marathon pace, your half marathon pace, 10 km pace, 5 km pace,

800 m pace and a 400 m sprint. Regardless of whether you run at these paces or not, everybody has them. After all, the pace that you complete your 400 m sprint at is faster than your 800 m effort, and that is faster than your 5 km effort, and so on. Few people develop awareness of these different paces and then utilise them in training, but failing to do so means they are not making the most of their training time.

This range of paces is often referred to as a zoned system, which you may have heard of. There are many different zoned systems, but they're all designed to do essentially the same thing. They are different ways to break your pace – from your warm-up pace through to your maximum pace – into different 'zones'. Sometimes placement of the zones changes slightly between systems, and sometimes the names of the zones change, but they all achieve the same outcome.

Given that we now know that the body adapts differently to different intensities, it becomes clear that we are going to have to run at different intensities within our training program to allow our body the stimulus it requires to adapt. Without placing our body under those training conditions, or stressors, it will not adapt. Naturally, a training program needs to be tailored for each distance. It is the mix of intensities and the timing of when a runner runs at these different intensities with respect to their personal capability and goal race that gives the ultimate outcome – being Run Fit and hitting regular PBs.

Timing and structuring the development of your fitness with respect to your goal event, plus the sequential progression of efforts that target different parts of your fitness, is a further layer required with periodization. This is why the training plan is the backbone of everything.

I know this all sounds a bit complicated, but as I said at the beginning of this section – there is no 'magic set'. If there is any magic involved in improving your run fitness, it is understanding how to use intensity. Different sets build different parts of your fitness based on the intensity at which you are running. Even so, runners often ask, 'What is the best run set that I need to complete to improve?' Unfortunately, there is no magic training set. It is blocks of training that deliver results. Undertaking quality training over and over again is the process that gives results. Week on week, race on race, year on year.

Now that I've convinced you that there is no magic set and no short cut to increased fitness, we will look at each of the three elements of your run fitness that you need to develop: your endurance, your speed and your strength.

## DEVELOP YOUR ENDURANCE

Aerobic endurance is the first part of fitness development that runners go to. It is your ability to use oxygen to create the energy needed to run. If you're better at doing this, you can run quicker between point A and point B. Specifically, what we are looking to develop here is your aerobic threshold. This is the point at which you transition from using oxygen to deliver energy to also creating lactate just above resting levels. As lactate levels start to increase you have moved from being able to generate enough energy through aerobic metabolism to creating energy using anaerobic pathways. If you are able to increase the point at which this occurs you will run faster between points A and B. You can simply say: 'I am fitter'.

Aerobic endurance development occurs best at a particular zone – a sweet spot, if you like. If you're running too slowly, then you are not taxing your aerobic system enough to create the stimulus it needs to adapt. When you run at pace zones well above your aerobic threshold you will maximally tax your aerobic system, but the time you can spend here is limited. This means the cumulative time spent training or taxing your aerobic zone is reduced. Both are mistakes that I see runners make regularly.

I had a runner called Lucas come to me for coaching. He was young and fit, and had found a zone system based on heart rate. He was following this system to ensure that he didn't complete his aerobic running at too high an effort. Upon starting to work with him, it quickly became apparent that he was indeed completing his aerobic running at a low effort – but that effort was far too low for him. We made sure that we determined exactly what his zones were, and as a result increased the effort level of his aerobic running. This created enough stimulus to force his aerobic system to adapt. The net result was that his run fitness started to improve, and he started to run quicker. Winning!

Some of the runners I coach have high aerobic threshold heart rates and others have low aerobic threshold heart rates. The key take-away here is that you need to determine what your personal heart rate, pace and power (if using) zones are so that your training is tailored to you. This is the key to developing your endurance.

## IMPROVE YOUR SPEED

While developing your aerobic engine has the net effect of increasing your running speed, when runners talk about improving their speed it's best to think about this as your race pace and quicker. Improving your running speed can happen in a variety of ways, many of which have already been covered. When we are discussing improving your speed with reference to your fitness, we are looking at improving your anaerobic threshold, VO2 max and neuromuscular ability.

Your anaerobic threshold, sometimes known as your lactate threshold, is a second threshold point. As your lactate levels continue to rise above your aerobic threshold (discussed on page 109) you continue to create energy using anaerobic pathways. We then reach a second threshold point, often known as the anaerobic threshold. This is the point at which lactate starts to increase more rapidly.

This is what you would know as your red line – it's when you are exercising hard and your body is completely flooded with lactate. At this point runners generally find that they can push harder but only for a short period of time before they're brought back to an effort that is just under their anaerobic threshold.

VO2 max, also known as aerobic capacity, is the maximum amount of oxygen an athlete can use from their blood in a minute. It is your maximum effort. An excruciating effort that you can only hold for very short periods of time. This point is well above your anaerobic threshold.

Finally, neuromuscular speed is about the ability of the muscles to contract simultaneously and forcefully. These types of coordinated contractions are needed to deliver high nerve impulses at just the right time so that the muscles can contract in the appropriate manner to move the body. If your body is better able to coordinate these impulses and provide a stronger impulse, the muscles are able to contract faster and with greater force, allowing you to run faster.

The distance of the race that you plan to tackle will determine the importance and extent to which you need to train these different areas. Shorter races will require greater training time to be spent on the VO2 max and neuromuscular speed, as opposed to longer races where aerobic and anaerobic threshold are more important.

Collectively all are important in the overall development of the runner. It is the timing, amount and balance between these areas that must be brought into the training program, that good old Game Plan, to deliver the best results for the individual runner and your chosen race distance. Like I said earlier – there is no magic set.

When it comes to running speed, I love to share the story of Kazu. It is a gorgeous story and illustrates many of the points that we have discussed earlier in the book, but is particularly useful to illustrate the point I have made about the speed side of things.

Kazu came to me after deciding to move from completing marathons to completing ultramarathons. She is a great runner and wanted to win the Yurrebilla Ultramarathon, South Australia's premier 56 km ultra, which is right in her backyard. Being the state's premier ultra, it always attracts a top-quality field of local and interstate runners. To add to the challenge, Yurrebilla was also to be Kazu's first ultra.

Kazu trained hard for the event and had an exceptional run, but unfortunately was beaten on the day by quality opposition. Not to be deterred, she decided she would enter the event again the following year. Her training was going beautifully; she was in great form leading in and primed to have another crack at achieving her goal. Then disaster struck. In her final long training run she rolled her ankle on the trail. After a trip to emergency she had two weeks to recover. While she wanted to run the event her ankle simply could not hold her weight on the downhills, and unfortunately she was a DNS (did not start). But Kazu's training and racing mindset is incredible. She recovered, rebuilt her running, and the following year again launched into a build for the race. In this third year Kazu was in a tight battle right to the final hill, but she managed to come out on top and achieve her goal of winning the event. To do this, she had to execute an exceptional race underpinned by her training and preparation in each of the areas we have discussed.

Of particular note was what we did with Kazu's speed work. As Kazu progressed with her running over the years, it became apparent that for her to win Yurrebilla she had to improve her anaerobic threshold. What proved to be the winning formula for her was to drop some of her aerobic volume to ensure she recovered well enough to tackle her high-quality speed sets, or what I personally like to call intensity sets. In these sets we pushed her anaerobic threshold again and again and again. This is mentally taxing training, but Kazu was up for the challenge and applied herself to the process. As you now know, it worked and allowed her to achieve her goal. Kazu is a Run Fit runner and damn did she finish with a smile.

## BUILD YOUR STRENGTH

Run strength is your ability to both control your body and exert a high force output for the duration of your event. To control your body means that you have the strength to maintain great run form for the duration of your event and the ability to withstand the ground reaction forces when you run. The ability to exert a high force output for the duration of the event is the ability to exert a high force onto the ground in order to propel yourself forward for the duration of the event. Run strength is particularly important over the final part of your event; if you have great run strength it allows you to finish well.

Let's first look at your ability to control your body. This is the ability for you to control your hips, forward lean and core, and have the leg strength to support your body. You need the strength to maintain appropriate hip position, which allows you to maintain appropriate lean, which allows you to control where your centre of gravity is for the duration of your event. You also need the strength to be able to handle the eccentric loading placed on your legs over the course of your event. Eccentric loading is the force that is placed on your legs when ground contact is made. To put these together we would say that you are able to maintain exceptional run form for the duration of your event.

The ability to withstand the ground reaction forces when you run is the ability to make contact with the ground at the impact phase of the run stride and control your foot, leg and body as this contact is made. The ability for you to control your body during the contact and loading phase to mid stance of the stride determines the speed at which you can move through to the take-off phase and progress into your next stride. When the body is dealing with these ground reaction forces, the muscles in the leg are lengthening under load. This is called an eccentric load. This type of loading is really fatiguing, and great strength is required for your muscles to be able to tolerate this load over and over again. In running this is happening in every single stride. If you are able to do this without fatiguing, we say you have great fatigue resistance.

If you have ever witnessed the finish of a marathon, or finished a marathon yourself, you may have noticed that when many runners come to the finish line they're cramping and unable to properly control their run form. This is often because of the eccentric load that they have been trying to tolerate over the course of the event. They have not built their run strength up to the point of being able to withstand these forces for the entire race. Under race conditions this regularly occurs from about the 30 km mark, when runners who have not trained properly are often forced to undertake the dreaded march to the finish line.

The second factor in building your run strength is to have a high force output for the duration of your event. This means that you can push back and down on the ground with a high force for the time taken to finish your race. This is the force needed to push you forward in your running, and it requires strength. If you have greater strength you are able to exert more force onto the ground, which in turn improves your stride length in the equation **Pace = Cadence x Stride Length**, which we looked at in Chapter 5. Again, you can start to appreciate how everything is interrelated and interconnected.

We can train your run strength both by running and through a run strength program. The best way to improve your run strength while running is to include hill work in your training, rather than always running on flat ground. This can include both uphill and downhill work, and this is as relevant to road runners as it is to trail runners. A run strength program may include an at-home routine using basic weights, such as a set of dumbbells, or it may be more advanced and include weights at a gym if the runner wishes. Which option works for the runner is a personal choice based on how much time they have and what their personal goals are.

While run strength is an essential part of improving your performance, it has the added benefit of reducing your injury risk. This is because that strength work increases the activation and recruitment of the muscles, can reduce and correct imbalances, and strengthens the connective tissue of the body. While strength has many performance benefits for the runner, it is because of its ability to help reduce injuries that I recommend runners complete at least one strength session each week.

I said at the start of this chapter that there is no magic set. Well, if you thought you could prepare for your goal event by just doing a lot of running, you now know that's wrong. Not only is there no magic running set, every now and then I want you to take your running shoes off and hit the weights instead of the road. I know you might not like the idea. I myself was incredibly reluctant to take on specific strength training as part of my training program, always arguing that I did it as part of my running with hill workouts. It took a lot of reflection to understand the reasoning behind my reluctance and fear, but I was finally able to identify the two main reasons why this was the case.

When I was younger, I had a poor experience with specific strength training and injured myself. While the injury was minor, it took me out of my beloved sport and meant I could not run. For me, it was a very powerful motivator *against* strength training. Secondly, because this injury happened early in my career, I didn't have a chance to experience the positive benefits that can come from a strength training program. Fortunately, I had a great physio who was able to introduce me to strength training in terms of rehab and injury prevention, and a very persistent partner who has a strength training background and who was able to fast-track my knowledge in this area.

I have gone from being a critic to being converted, and now I'm a preacher of strength training benefits. I include both run strength training and specific strength training as part of my weekly training program. If you come to strength training with apprehension as I did, be open to working with a quality strength trainer or coach to help develop your knowledge in this area.

## CONCLUSION

Your fitness development is now under control. You know that if you put your body into a state of quality training repetitively, it will adapt. You are aware that there are no magic sets and it is blocks of training, week on week, month on month and year on year, that will deliver results.

You also know that there are three elements of fitness which need your focus as a runner: endurance, speed and strength. Taking the time to develop each of these at the right time and in the right way, relative to the timing and distance of your goal race, is vital to allow the body all the wonderful adaptations that occur with training.

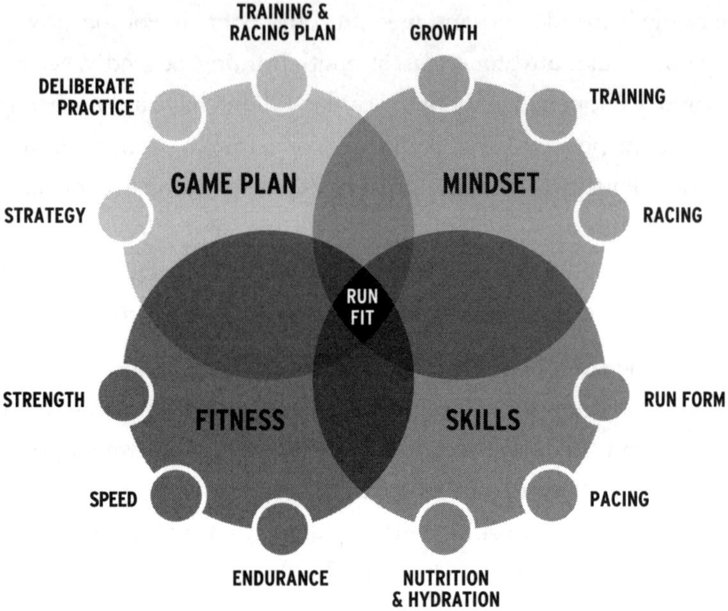


You have now covered the complete Run Fit Method – go you! You now have the fundamental knowledge needed to improve your running and finish with a smile. To summarise your knowledge, the Run Fit Method is made up of four key components: the Game Plan, Mindset, Skills and Fitness. Each of these has three key areas requiring your focus and attention. For the Game Plan, those areas are a strategy, deliberate practice, and a training and racing plan. Mindset is made up of developing a growth mindset and enhancing your training and racing mindset. The skills you need include improving your run form and pacing, and mastering your nutrition and hydration. Finally, your fitness comprises your ability to develop your endurance, speed and strength.

Phew, what a journey so far. But we have one final, vital topic to cover – Run Fit in action. We need to look at Run Fit Coaching and getting Run Fit.

## YOUR JOURNEY

If you're keen to know more about the Run Fit Method, book into one of our online Run Fit Workshops where we unpack the Game Plan, Mindset, Skills and Fitness in more detail.

Details can be found on our website
www.therunjourney.com/workshop

**PART 3**

# RUN FIT IN ACTION

Run Fit in Action dives into two key elements to becoming Run Fit – staying on track and putting someone in your corner to assist you. When you get started it can be hard to find motivation and figure out how to fit running into your life, so we'll take a look at how to do that. We also need to make sure that you do not derail your training. Unfortunately many runners do derail their training through those dreaded running injuries, so we will look at how to make sure you don't become a statistic. Specifically we will look at run load and develop our understating of how long it takes the body to adapt to training. Following this we will look at why you should get a coach and what holds many runners back from doing so. We will cover how a coach can unlock endless improvement for you and discover the secret ingredients of coaching. As we round the final corner, we can hear the crowd cheering and see the finish arch coming into focus. So stay strong – success is in sight.

CHAPTER 7

# STAYING ON TRACK

*Being broken doesn't win*

We spent the first part of this book looking at the profound power of running and how it can change your life. We thought about why you run and made sure you were tuned in to what truly motivates you. Then we looked at basic Run Fit principles so you can understand why your running has to be developed in certain ways and what makes a quality, sustainable training program. In Part 2 you had a crash course on the four elements of the Run Fit Method. You now have a vast amount of knowledge, and you're ready to hit the road. Surely you can't possibly fail!

But as you hit the road and begin running for the first time, or progress your capability from basic or intermediate into something more advanced, you need to take care. Any runner can find themselves struck by Run Fit Derailment, especially if they become impatient, lose focus or fail to take proper care of themselves. In this chapter we're going to look at some of the obstacles that you might encounter as you move towards becoming Run Fit, so that you can be prepared and be patient.

## CREATE GOOD HABITS

Success doesn't happen by luck or chance; you have to work to be your best. One of the best ways to work towards success is to break bad habits and create positive ones. The best way to break a bad habit is to swap it for a good one. If you have a bad habit of lying on the couch after work, you need to swap it for a better habit – running. If you always run too hard over the start of a race or training set, you need to swap it with a better habit – pacing yourself.

As Aristotle said, 'We are what we repeatedly do. Excellence then is not an act but a habit.' To build positive run habits is your first objective once you launch your Game Plan. It makes sense that to be a better runner we are going to have to spend some time running. By putting in place a structure we are able to build your run habits.

Sometimes it's hard to get started, but be patient. Positive run habits are achieved over time. Steady, gradual improvement is the path to success. If you're a new runner, we might start you on two runs per week before progressing you to three runs per week. Likewise we might consolidate with a runner who runs three times per week before progressing them to four runs per week. Change happens slowly so that you can succeed.

It takes about twenty-eight days for a change to become normal. Until that time, it's an arm wrestle, but after it becomes normal it becomes easy because it's your new habit – it's simply what you do. Soon, you don't even have to think about finding motivation to get out the door.

Even so, if you miss a day, or goof up something you're trying to change, that's okay. You are changing, you are growing, you are allowed to make mistakes. If it was easy it wouldn't be worth it. So what do you do? You keep going and aim to do better the next day. And again, and again and again, until you do succeed. That is how the best work to be their best. That is following the process. You guessed it – that is being a Run Fit runner.

## HOW TO FIT RUNNING INTO YOUR LIFE

If you're serious about this running caper, you need commitment. You need to find a way to fit running into your life. Unfortunately, many runners have an illusion of limited time. They say, 'I can't achieve my running goals... I don't have time.' I would argue that you do have time. But perhaps you think you need to do more running than you actually do to achieve your goals. You certainly don't have to run every day of the week, but yes, you will have to run. Building up to three or four runs per week allows most runners to achieve their goals. While others certainly do run more – five, six or seven times per week – this is not always required. Running more frequently is a decision they have made because they want to dedicate more time to running. But the illusion of not having time to fit in three runs per week that benefit your health, wellness, vitality and productivity? That I question.

The best way to overcome your doubts about fitting running into your life is to simply start. Start with fitting in one small run per week and build from there. The same concept applies for someone wanting to add an extra run to their week. Start with one extra run but keep it small and build in the habit. This will create momentum and you will be amazed at what you can achieve and where it will take you.

If kids are part of the scene, they can complicate things. But that is okay. I am yet to meet a runner who, with guidance, can't fit work, family *and* running in. There are many ways to build out a training plan and many ways to achieve the desired result. Many runners love the day when their kids are old enough and start to come with them on their training runs. Why should you have all the fun? And when you race, friends and family can come along and share the experience so you can have quality time with one another.

Remember, however, that you need to fit running into your life, not your life into your running. Running is important, but it is not your whole life. If it is, you're not a whole person. You need balance. Balance between family, work and running. Sometimes runners start on a run training program and don't keep flexibility in what they do. Work commitments come up, family commitments encroach, and suddenly they find that they're ill or fatigue builds up. But they try to keep their run plan rigid. Remember that there is always flexibility in the run program and you need to be adaptable. This may mean shifting your run days slightly or getting up early instead of running in the afternoon, or vice versa. Remember that we want to form great habits, but we want to have flexibility when needed.

As long as we adhere to basic training principles when moving our run program around, there is always scope to fit your running comfortably into your life. That is indeed the beauty and freedom of a sport that you only need a pair of shoes to undertake.

## AN OUNCE OF PREVENTION

So, we've got you up and running – literally! You've found your mojo, found a way to fit your running into your life, and started to consolidate your new habits. But what if getting started wasn't your problem? What if you have too much enthusiasm? Now it's time to talk about that elephant sitting there in the middle of the room – injuries. Or what I like to call 'run fit derailment'.

Runners are injured far too regularly. The statistics are shocking. On average '70% of recreational and competitive runners sustain overuse injuries during any 12-month period'.[7] To be injured is the opposite of being Run Fit. Injury limits your running, or can even stop it altogether. When this happens you lose your freedom and your identity, and everything you have worked so hard for starts to go backwards. It's no wonder an injured runner is a grumpy runner.

It is important that we understand exactly what a running injury is. The following is a handy definition: 'Running-related (training or competition) musculoskeletal pain in the lower limbs that causes a restriction or stoppage of running (distance, speed, duration or training) for at least seven days or three consecutive scheduled training sessions, or that requires the runner to consult a physician or other health professional.'[8]

Sometimes injuries are unavoidable. Any runner can roll an ankle, slip and fall in their driveway, or have an accident in their everyday

7 https://sma.org.au/resources-advice/running/

8 *A Consensus Definition of Running Related Injury in Recreational Runners: A Modified Delphi Approach*, https://www.jospt.org/doi/pdf/10.2519/jospt.2015.5741, accessed 24 November 2020

life which impacts their running. But many running injures *are* avoidable. It's important to focus on what we can control, so let's look at preventable injuries. Preventable injuries include iliotibial band friction syndrome (ITB), plantar fasciitis, stress fractures, shin splints, patellofemoral pain syndrome (runner's knee) and patellar tendinopathy.

Many preventable injuries are caused by overuse. Overuse injuries can occur from training errors with regard to running frequency, duration, distance and speed. Lack of leg strength and flexibility may be a factor. Overuse injuries may also be caused by inappropriate surfaces, terrain and footwear. We must be aware that training errors and therefore overuse injuries are more common than acute (sudden) injuries, such as a rolled ankle.[9]

## YOUR JOURNEY

What run injuries have you had in the past? List them below.

Next to them mark 'A' for acute (rolled ankle, slip and fall, etc.) or 'O' for overuse (ITB, plantar fasciitis, runner's knee, shin splints or patellar tendinopathy) to get a feel for where improvements can be made.

- 
- 
- 

9 https://sma.org.au/resources-advice/running/

## RUN LOAD - THE KEY TO SAFE TRAINING

Now that we understand that many running injuries are preventable, let's look at how to avoid them. To do this, we first have to understand run load and the way in which the body adapts. These two concepts go hand in hand, and will give you the required knowledge to allow you to avoid most injuries and put steps in place to minimise their effect if and when you feel a niggle.

Run load is the combined effect of all the running stress you are putting on your body. Run load comprises the frequency that you run, the intensity at which you run, and the time spent running. And as you may know, together those factors create the term FIT.

To quickly recap: **frequency** refers to how often you run. **Intensity** refers to how hard you are running. **Time** refers to the time spent running. If you increase any of these factors – run more often, run harder or run for longer – you have increased your run load and your body has to adapt and come back stronger. Collectively, these factors combine over weeks, months and years to allow a runner to progress their run load. While most runners understand this principle, many runners and even coaches still apply the principle incorrectly.

Run stress is essential, as stressing the body is what allows it to adapt and come back stronger, but far too many runners go in with a short-term focus and stress the body too far too quickly. They rush the process and increase the intensity, time or frequency of their runs too quickly. Or worse, they increase all three factors simultaneously without considering each as part of the collective whole.

The penalty for this impatience is an injury, which puts them further back in their running than they were before they started. When this happens they need to rehab their injury, then take the time to progress to the point they were at before they were injured. Only then can they continue on their journey to reach their full potential.

If you're still not convinced that slow progression is safer progression, let's look at injuries and recovery time. As a very rough guide, a muscle injury is going to take 1–12 weeks to rehab, a tendon or ligament injury is going to take 3–6 months to rehab, and a bone injury is going to take 3–12 months to rehab. These timeframes are very approximate, but you can see that a bone generally takes longer to rehab than a tendon or ligament, and a tendon or ligament takes longer than a muscle. This rehab time is dictated by the rate at which cells in these tissues take to regenerate or be replaced and come back stronger.

Understanding how long it takes for muscles, tendons and bones to regenerate and come back stronger helps us understand the time frames our body needs to adapt to the stress caused by running. We need to allow our body time to adapt, yet runners simply don't do this. They find that their fitness improves, so they run more often, harder and for longer – and then they break.

Many then enter a spiral that I like to call the injury, run, injury cycle. They get injured, then start running again and find it's all going well so they increase their run load. But they do this too quickly and end up injured again. This cycle then repeats. Sometimes it's the same injury, sometime it's the same injury but on the opposite side of their body, and sometimes it's a new injury. It's a vicious cycle that demoralises a runner. They wonder if they are simply not meant to run and question whether running is for them.

What's happening here is that their body is becoming deconditioned and can't handle what they want it to do. The runner's reference point for what they think they can do may be too high, because often they're in the best run form of their life just before they have their first injury. They need to slow down and find the cause of the problem before moving on. Rehab once and rehab right.

This is why we need to treat you like an apple tree and slowly, steadily and gradually build up your running. I have worked with many a broken runner. I have had runners come to me with stress fractures, shin splints and torn calves, to name just a few injuries. First I have to progress them through the stages of injury rehab with appropriate professionals such as physiotherapists. Only then can we slowly build up their running body to the point that it can handle what they think is a respectable run load. This is hard, and I often find I'm pulling the runner back, putting on the handbrake and taking things slower than they would like. But fast forward six to twelve months when they hit their best running, and they're so glad that I made them take it slowly.

You may be wondering what this looks like in action. Mandy came to me after having had two stress fractures. She rehabbed from the first stress fracture and gradually built her run load back to the point where she was confident and hired a run coach to assist. She followed the program that was outlined for her and then she encountered her second stress fracture – this time on the opposite leg. She progressed through her rehab for a second time, at which point she gave me a call. I asked a few questions, looking to establish the cause of the first and second injury. It was obvious what the problem was – she had increased her run load too quickly. Especially after the first injury. Her frequency was up, her time spent running was up, her intensity was up. Not only was her run load up, it was excessive – all under the guidance of a run coach! There are right ways to do things and wrong ways. In this case every rule had been broken. No wonder she had a second stress fracture. I was infuriated at the coach; Mandy deserved better.

After pulling things back and putting the right process in place, Mandy progressed. Slowly, steadily and surely. Her run load was managed with an appropriate Game Plan, and frequency, intensity and time spent running were all carefully controlled. From 30 km a week, to 35 km a week, to 40 km a week through to an 80 km week. Mandy has been enjoying her running again for over a year, is back completing the ultramarathons she loves and couldn't be happier. Mandy is now a Run Fit runner and running with a smile.

## YOUR JOURNEY

Consider your injury list on page 128. Did you determine the cause of the injury yourself or with the assistance of a health care professional or a run coach? If you determined that the injury was run load related, let's make sure we have learned from the past and put in place steps to ensure this doesn't happen again.

## WHEN PREVENTION IS NOT ENOUGH

While we want to avoid injuries, if they do strike, we need to know what to do. First and foremost, we need to seek assistance. This could be medical care or guidance from a coach. While this may sound obvious, many runners continue to run on an injury and exacerbate it. By seeking assistance early, we can modify a run training program to allow the body to recover. This may mean that you can still run, but in a reduced capacity. If the injury is more significant, it may require time off from running and a significant modification to your training as you gradually rebuild your running load.

There are two key questions I ask with every injured runner I work with.

1. What is the diagnosis?
2. What was the cause?

It's essential to answer both these questions. The value of taking the time to do a thorough diagnosis cannot be underestimated. Without this step you could be putting in place the wrong rehab protocol. Muscles, tendons and bone all require different rehab. Getting the correct diagnosis at the start means the right steps are taken from the start. In short, this means you get back out running sooner.

Once you have a diagnosis, you can look for the cause of the injury. Knowing how the injury was caused allows you to put in place measures to avoid being injured in the same way again.

And finally – do your rehab work. Not many runners find the rehab fun, but attack it with a positive mindset and get it done.

## RECOVERY IS PART OF THE PLAN

Recovery is often forgotten by runners. They focus on the running part – the training. When you're training you are breaking your body down. You are damaging the muscle fibres, causing them to break. You are building up toxic by-products in the blood stream and cells. But this damage has to be repaired. And it is at rest that your body repairs itself. This is what allows it to come back stronger. This part is often forgotten by runners. Without recovery, your body would be a crumpled mess. This is why it is essential to include recovery in any quality training program. Recovery can be lighter training days or complete days off. Many runners are reluctant to 'take it easy', but when you shift your mindset to seeing recovery as part of the plan – and that it aids you in achieving everything you want from running – these days suddenly become important.

Let me illustrate the point. Earlier in the book we looked at why you run. Let's say you decided that your reasons were to run a marathon for the first time or to set a PB in the marathon. That means you're going to have to run a lot. But we need to understand that there is a point at which we are running too much. If you complete one or more training runs above your ideal run load, you risk ending up with an injury. Does this put you closer to or further from your goal? Clearly you are now further from achieving that goal. If we understand our 'why', it makes it easy to decide when recovery is needed, how much is needed and when you need to listen to your body. It helps you keep your eyes on the prize. This means we can really enjoy easier run days because we understand that they're important in the bigger picture. You won't feel guilty when you take days off from running, because you know they allow your body to repair so you can run faster tomorrow and ultimately achieve your goals.

You can't be on your 'A Game' all the time. Over the year your body can handle times of higher loading leading to an increase in fitness. But if we try to maintain that state endlessly, the body never enters a prolonged state of repair. A prolonged state of repair certainly does not mean that you are not training – you absolutely are – it is simply that we are in a maintenance phase. More than anything, this is for the mind. To allow the mind to relax, reconnect with your love of running and rebuild the hunger for your next great running experience or race. The runner who struggles is the one who jumps from one race to the next without taking any down time. If you break your mind and kill your love of running, then you have lost. Being broken doesn't win.

## CONCLUSION

You have now embarked on the path to becoming Run Fit. But you know that it takes time to consolidate your habits and are aware that you need to fit running into your life, not your life into your running. You have bypassed the misconception of limited time that holds many runners back from achieving their dreams and know you simply have to start. You also understand that we need to avoid injuries at all cost as these undermine the very essence of being a Run Fit runner. You have a solid appreciation of run load and the parts of the FIT principle that contribute to this. You have looked at your past injuries to determine the causes and know what to do if injury strikes again. Finally, you understand the importance of recovery. You now have the underpinning knowledge to ensure you avoid run fit derailment.

CHAPTER 8

# RUN FIT COACHING

*'When the student is ready the teacher will appear.'*

ANONYMOUS

We're nearing the end of our journey together. Or are we? You may think you have all the knowledge required to become a Run Fit runner after reading this book, but there is one more area I want to discuss. As you continue on your journey, don't think you have to go it alone. Run Fit Coaching is about putting someone in your corner who can guide you in implementing all that has been discussed with the Run Fit Method so that you can become Run Fit. In this chapter we're going to discuss a progression that new runners frequently take, why you should get a coach, the biggest reason people don't get a coach, and how having a run coach works.

## THE RUNNER'S PROGRESSION

The runner's progression often goes something like this...

Someone decides they want to become a runner and start running. That is a great first step. But without knowledge or fitness backing them, what many runners do is simply start to run as far as they can once a week. Then they decide that next week they're going to run as far as they can again, which will be a bit further than the week before, and then a bit further again. This continues for a period of time. Slowly they get fitter, and some now have enough confidence to enter races like parkrun.

Their training continues and they slowly improve. But they want to improve more quickly. This is where things pick up pace. They learn that if they move from running once a week to twice a week, and then three times a week, their improvement not only continues but speeds up. Some break down and injure themselves at this point. Those who don't discover that if they go hard when they run, their fitness improves at a faster rate. So now they complete each run as hard as they can. They're now running as hard as they can two or three times a week. Then one of two things then happens; they injure themselves or their performance plateaus.

Now they're in danger of going down the path of the disheartened runner – a runner who, once they lose their first flush of enthusiasm, begins to struggle. A runner who is injured or injured regularly. Who loses the joy in their running. Who lacks confidence and clarity in what they're doing. They run a bit here and run a bit there, sometimes they're motivated and at other times they're not. They have a bunch of events they would like to do, but there is no clear direction on how to get there. They simply go for a run. And sometimes go for a run more often. There is no variety in what they're doing. They wonder why they don't improve while runners around them do. They're caught in a form slump. Initially training was easy, but slowly and surely they have found themselves in a rut, burnt out and unmotivated by what they used to love.

There are many right ways to train as a runner and there are many ways that training can be done better. I started to get into running when I left school, and I used to do many of the things described above. I would bound out the door, jog the 200 m to the end of my street as my warm-up, and then complete my gorgeous run loop along the river where I lived. This started as a slow jog, progressed to running hard over the final section and then, you guessed it, completing the whole loop as fast as I could – full gas! This would bring me back to the top of my street where I would then jog the 200 m home as a warm down. Run over – a total of 3 km. I even recall making a time chart on my wall of how long each run took as I tried to improve and set a PB over my course… every time.

I now look back on those early running days and smile. Many runners progress in a similar way when they first start running. But my regimen, while it seemed legitimate, meant my performance was limited and I saw limited improvements. I was also in danger of being injured. Had that happened, I may well have gone down the track of becoming one of the disheartened runners described above. Fortunately, two important things happened that prevented me from losing my mojo and becoming a disheartened runner.

Not long after I began running I started university and commenced a Bachelor of Applied Science Human Movement (Exercise and Sports Science). I also joined the Lakers Triathlon club, where I found many great mentors and coaches. Both these experiences allowed me to fast-track my knowledge. When I finally entered a structured run program, underpinned by sound training principles, I fell in love with the process of training and improvement. Had I done this earlier, my rate of improvement would have gone through the roof, but most importantly, I would have enjoyed the training even more.

Fortunately I was open to this change in my routine, and I certainly hope you are too. I don't want you to become a disheartened runner, and one of the best ways to avoid that is to get a coach.

## WHY GET A COACH?

I always find it interesting to ask people what they would do if they wanted to learn the piano or play tennis. More often than not they say, 'Oh, I'd get a music teacher,' or 'I'd get a tennis coach.' Why then, when I ask people if they would like to learn how to run, do they not say, 'Oh, I'd get a run coach'? Instead they simply say, 'I'd go and run.' Please pause and consider this before reading on.

There are many reasons to get a run coach, but to sum it up a run coach can allow you to achieve your goal of becoming Run Fit faster and more easily while enjoying the process more along the way. Just like me when I first started running, you can't know what you don't know. But a run coach has that knowledge. A run coach can put in place a structured and detailed plan, reduce or mitigate your risk of injury, allow you to consistently improve your performance over a period of years, increase training variety and, above all, help you to enjoy your running more. So why are so many people still resistant to the idea?

I have come to the conclusion that the difference here lies in what we discussed in the first chapter. The difference between running to exercise and running to train. What often happens is that people who run for exercise start to train, which is fantastic, but they do not change their thought process and recognise this difference.

Training Peaks conducted an informal survey of its users and found the top seven reasons athletes like to work with a coach were: accountability, structure, smarts, reduced risk of over-training, motivation, time management, and so they don't have to do the thinking.[10] I would add – if you don't work with a coach, what are you leaving on the table? How much better could you be? How much more would you be able to challenge yourself and push your comfort zones? How much more fun could you have as you complete different runs, different races and different training? How much more adventure could you have with your running by changing where you run, going on running camps and travelling locally, interstate and internationally with your running? Working with a run coach opens up possibilities with your running that you probably never considered. So what's stopping you? Let's take a look at that.

## BUT I'M NOT GOOD ENOUGH FOR A COACH

I have learned that once runners decide that a coach could help them, the thing that holds them back is fear. Fear that they are not good enough. They start to run, and plan to get a coach once they're good enough. This is a pet hate of mine. I have lost count of how many times runners have done this and then injured themselves as they 'got themselves fit enough' to feel worthy of run coaching.

To go back to my earlier analogy, this is the equivalent of someone getting a tennis coach after they have learned to play tennis. The best tennis players in the world had a tennis coach when they were

10 http://www.trainingpeaks.com/blog/the-top-7-reasons-to-work-with-a-coach/

learning to play the game, and continue to have a tennis coach when they're among the best at what they do. It's simply that the dynamic of how the coach operates changes.

You are worthy now and you will always be worthy. Run coaching is not only for the elite; it is for you to achieve your best. Start now, for all the reasons I have mentioned above. You will love it and never look back.

## UNCONSCIOUS INCOMPETENCE TO CONSCIOUS COMPETENCE

When you decide to train with a coach, there is a progression that you are likely to take – a better progression than the one we talked about at the beginning of this chapter, which so often ends in injured and unhappy runners. Let's talk about that for a moment.

With running and sports there are right ways to do things and principles to follow, and also wrong ways to do things. When you improve at something, you always progress through the following four steps:

1. unconscious incompetence
2. conscious incompetence
3. conscious competence
4. unconscious competence

### Unconscious Incompetence

You don't know you're doing 'it' wrong, but a skilled performer can quickly tell you that 'it' is just wrong.

### Conscious Incompetence

You now realise you're doing 'it' wrong, often because you've been told by a teacher, coach or skilled performer. But you continue to complete the activity in the incorrect manner because that's the way you have always done it.

### Conscious Competence

You have now corrected the mistake, but have to think about it every time to perform 'it' correctly.

### Unconscious Competence

You have now corrected the mistake and do 'it' correctly every time without thinking, because this is now the way you do things.

Each of us has areas where we are highly skilled and areas where we are novices and would benefit from learning from others. My role as a running coach is to allow people to progress quickly, easily and with joy through these learning stages so they can become Run Fit.

## THE 1% RULE

Runners come to me to get Run Fit. That means they want to improve. If I were to talk in percentages and ask someone if they wanted to improve by one per cent, they probably wouldn't think that was all that exciting. But if I were to ask if they would like to improve their running by ten per cent, they would surely answer, 'Oh yes!' As a coach, it's the one per centers that count.

One per cent isn't much, barely makes a difference and is quite easy to achieve. On the other hand, ten per cent improvement creates a noticeable difference but may be difficult to achieve. The trick is to make a one per cent difference ten or more times, continuously. Then you have not just a ten per cent improvement, but continuous improvement. An improvement that, if you tried to make it in just one area, would seem impossible.

How do I get these results? I certainly don't make a ten per cent difference in one area instantaneously. I aim to make a one per cent difference regularly, repetitively and across a range of areas.

I make a...

1% improvement in your strategy

1 % improvement in your racing plan

1% improvement in your training sets

1 % improvement in your growth mindset

1% improvement in your training mindset

1 % improvement in your racing mindset

1 % improvement in your run form

1 % improvement in your pacing

1 % improvement in your nutrition and hydration

1 % improvement in your endurance

1 % improvement in your speed

1 % improvement in your strength

We're already at twelve per cent, and I'm just getting started – this list is far from exhaustive. I improve your running regularly, repetitively and across a range of areas. And then repeat this again and again. That is how a Run Fit runner improves their running week on week, month on month and year on year, and you can do it too.

## WHAT TO EXPECT FROM COACHING

The training programs that I set up for runners take into account all that has been discussed so far. In the coaching process we review, implement and work on the elements outlined in the Run Fit Method so you can improve your running and finish with a smile.

That means that the training sets you complete have deliberate practice built into them and the sets follow current best practice. It means you are able to ask questions and get feedback on how your running is going. You are able to implement the race plan. You are able to review training sets and races. It's like having a personal trainer for your running. Runners love the process and especially the results they see.

The best thing is that you can be anywhere in the world and achieve these results. I live in Adelaide, Australia, and I certainly do coach runners locally, but I also coach runners from interstate and overseas. I'm able to leverage technology, specifically online training software, to put in place Run Fit Plans. I guide and teach people all over the world how to run.

In the software you can track your fitness month on month and year on year. This becomes incredibly insightful. The software also allows us to use built-in features to look at a range of graphs on how your training is going, either in an individual set or over time.

We're able to check that we are progressing, and if we're not, we can immediately make changes so that we are.

A great example of remote training comes from Lisa, a runner I coach who lives in Europe. Distance has been no barrier to improving her running, which we have been able to improve year on year for three years. She loves the structure her training plan brings to her life, and she tells me she can now run up hills she was never able to run up before, and is now quicker than running friends who used to have to wait for her. We were able to achieve this by ensuring solid communication was in place. We communicate through the inbuilt message tool in the coaching software, send emails as needed and schedule video calls when required. I can see where she runs and how her runs went. I can plan runs based on this feedback and ensure that each element of the Run Fit method is in place for Lisa. I provide feedback and guidance on her running and plan her runs to fit in with her work and life commitments. She absolutely loves the structure her training brings to her life and couldn't be happier with her running. Lisa is a Run Fit runner.

## YOUR JOURNEY

Log on now to set up a Training Peaks account at **www.trainingpeaks.com**. The basic version is completely free and lets you start collecting all your data, which gives great insight into where your running is currently at.

## THE SECRET INGREDIENTS OF COACHING

I am often asked how my coaching differs from other run coaches. Well, I do have a few secret ingredients...

The first secret ingredient of good coaching is communication. It's what allows feedback, review and analysis of your training and your understanding of training principles. It's how your questions can be answered. Communication is what allows you to implement training principles correctly and apply them to yourself. Communication helps us to make the little tweaks to your training that make all the difference. It's the certainty that you get when you're confident in what you are doing. There is an old saying, 'Give a man a fish and you feed him for a day. Teach a man to fish and you feed him for a lifetime.' Communication is how we teach you to train and how a coach can help you to become Run Fit for a lifetime.

Good coaching is about the runner having the confidence to communicate when necessary. Coupled with this is the feedback that coaches can provide athletes. Changes to training in response to frequent feedback may be subtle, but it is these tweaks here and there that make all the difference. Remember the 1% rule? Slowly and surely these tweaks compound to gradually shift and improve a runner's training. The athlete has confidence because they know a coach has their back. Not all coaches provided this feedback in an ongoing manner, but rather leave the runner to their own devices to make best guess attempts to improve. But that's not the way I do things. Communication is integral to the Run Fit Method.

I always include deliberate practice when I coach, which is built into the training sets and is a technique that few run coaches employ.

This is a skill that has been refined and learned over many years, and which I continue to develop so that I can plan and program pertinent training sets for runners. You are unlikely to find this anywhere else.

My background in education is also something that few coaches bring to the table. I embed the education of you, the athlete, in all that I do. This is central to my coaching philosophy for making you a better runner. This comes through in my method and my manner. It is central to how I guide, assist and coach.

Finally, I am the only coach using the Run Fit Method described in this book. It is my method entirely. Taking a holistic and rounded approach to improving your running, ensuring that nothing is left on the table and you can continue to improve in all the essential areas and elements – that's 100% unique and something you cannot get anywhere else.

## CONCLUSION

You now understand Run Fit Coaching. You're familiar with the way that runners typically progress when they start to run, and you understand why you should get a run coach. You are also aware that fear often holds people back from getting a run coach but that this fear is not warranted. You are already good enough as you are, and a run coach can help accelerate your journey to being a Run Fit runner. You also know the 1% rule and how improving by one per cent in a range of areas leads to endless improvement. Finally, you have learned about the secret ingredients of coaching – communication, deliberate practice, education and the Run Fit Method.

# GET RUN FIT

This book has taken us on a journey together. We started by covering the Run Fit philosophy. Then we looked at a set of guiding principles that help us become Run Fit runners. Next we dived into the Run Fit Method. A method to allow you to improve your running and finish with a smile. Following this we looked at what to expect when you launch your Run Fit adventure, and finally we covered Run Fit Coaching.

You now know the principles and fundamentals needed to be Run Fit. If you haven't done so while you've been reading this book, it's now time to begin your journey to becoming Run Fit. I really urge you to get up and do something, now that you have the knowledge to make a change, because far too many people don't change what they do. They understand the method, they want to improve, and then they do nothing. Let's make sure that's not you. You have the knowledge, but knowledge is not power – it is potential power. This knowledge gives you a competitive advantage against the rest of the field, but it's up to you to use it.

If you implement the Run Fit Method, your best running is in front of you. It takes time to become a great runner, but with the right method now in place you can achieve that success. Few runners have a holistic approach and so never reach their full potential. We have now changed that. Regardless of your age, your best running is still to come and you can enjoy running for life. This means improving PBs, run adventures, camps, run holidays and new friendships born out of running.

At the start of this book I made a big audacious promise. One that I come back to.

Run Fit runners are the ones who improve their running and finish with a smile. They train with confidence, clarity and focus. They are injury free; they love the process of training and the structure it brings to their life. They have confidence in what they're doing. They thrive on the experiences that training and completing or competing in various events brings. They love the challenge and journey of improving and are driven to improve. They have certainty on the start line that they are going to have a fantastic experience and enjoy the day out. They finish with a smile, hit PBs and are already dreaming of their next running adventure. Running brings them abundant happiness. Running is their way of life.

The promise you make, and the promise all the runners I work with make to me is: that they will follow their training plan to the best of their ability. Run, implement, learn, grow and succeed. The promise I make to all the runners I work with is simple: I will be the best coach that I can be. I will do everything in my power to make them the best runner they can be. It's powerful, it works and it gets results. The question is: are you trying to go it alone or have you made a promise? Make a promise to become a Run Fit runner and finish with a smile.

As you progress on your running journey, there are several resources that can support you in becoming a Run Fit runner. Turn the page to learn more.

# NEXT STEPS

## THE RUN FIT SCORECARD

Take the Run Fit Scorecard. The questions are designed to score you on the four areas required to become Run Fit as described in this book. It gives you a personalised report, which can be used to fast-track your improvement. Take the scorecard at www.therunjourney.com/scorecard. It will take about 5–10 minutes.

## THE RUN FIT WORKSHOP

Book in for a Run Fit online workshop. If you're keen to know more about the Run Fit Method, you will benefit from our online Run Fit Workshops where we unpack the Game Plan, Mindset, Skills and Fitness in more detail and you can ask any questions you may have.

Details can be found on our website
www.therunjourney.com/workshop

## THE RUN FIT CLUB

To improve your chances of success, you need to surround yourself with people who normalise what you do and what you want to achieve. You can do that by finding a runner or runners who are great training partners. And you don't even have to run side by side.

The Run Fit Club is an online club that I developed, which allows you to be part of a group of individuals who are committed to your success. It's a community of runners who love running, love learning about running and love improving their running. The club is built around allowing you to implement the principles and methods discussed in this book. You receive a detailed training plan based on your personal race choice: 5 km, 10 km, half marathon, marathon, etc. We will also take into account your ability level: new runner, beginner, intermediate or advanced. There is also weekly coach feedback, online run workshops, training set reviews, accountability, and a range of videos explaining how to use the Run Fit Method on the members-only website.

Runners usually join for three to twelve months to target one or two races, but often retain their membership after their first year and decide to tackle a series of races. As discussed earlier, you may be a new runner tackling a 5 km run, or a beginner wanting to tackle a 10 km and then half marathon. Others want to tackle the marathon and others a 50 km and then a 100 km ultramarathon. This is completely up to you and your audacious running goals. The club lets you learn and implement Run Fit with myself and others on the weekly Coach Talk. Runners love jumping on to learn from other people's questions – often questions they had not considered. It increases your motivation and lets you develop great run habits, which in turn creates fantastic momentum with your running.

Join the Run Fit Club by heading to www.therunjourney.com/run-fit-club. Use the code RunFit to unlock your free two-week trial.

See you there.

# RUN FIT CLUB

Finish with a smile.

## THE PROBLEM

- No structured training plan
- Injured now or regularly
- Performance plateau (No PB in 12 months)
- No training variety

**Detailed run training plan** | **Weekly coach feedback** | **Online Run Workshops**

### GAME PLAN

Run with focus

Training clarity

Enjoy the journey

### MINDSET

Build momentum

Stay motivated

Build racing & training resilience

### SKILLS

Improved run form

Nutrition & hydration

Master pacing

### FITNESS

Develop your engine

Increased speed

Become a stronger runner

**Training Set Reviews** | **Accountability** | **Membership Videos**

12 MONTHS

## RUN FIT

- Structured training plan
- Injury free
- Run improvement (Finish with a 20–60 minute PB)
- Training variety

**THE WHAT**

The Run Fit Club provides the focus guidance and accountability that drives the ability for you to get Run Fit

**ADVENTURE**

**THE PRIZE**

Train with confidence, improve your running, enjoy the journey, finish with a smile

**CHALLENGE**

**OUR WHY**

We exist to help runners enjoy the experience, journey and joy of running for life

**FUN**

## RUN FIT PERSONAL ONLINE COACHING – WANT TO BE COACHED BY ME?

For those who prefer the one-on-one approach to coaching, I offer personal implementation of the Run Fit Method. I guide runners through the process of becoming Run Fit, ensuring all areas and components are developed. Due to the intensive nature of this coaching, only limited places are available. It is also worth noting here that while ability is not a barrier to whether I coach someone, having a growth mindset is. Most of the runners who I work with have never been coached before and have never been on a structured run training plan. They are beginner runners new to formal, structured run training. But many of the runners I coach go on to become intermediate and advanced runners. Like them, you have to be willing to implement the training plan and guidance that is put in place. You have to be open to changing and improving what you do so that you can achieve the success that you desire. I can't run for you, but if you are prepared to run and do the hard work, I can get you Run Fit.

Email info@therunjourney.com with your name, goal event and why you would like me to coach you and we will let you know more details.

You could be like one of the runners I have mentioned in this book, with your own success story to tell your friends and family. But don't take my word for it – turn the page to see what the runners are saying. Runners just like you.

# TESTIMONIALS

## KAREN HEATH

I am new to running and was really unsure about getting a running coach. Not being fast I thought, 'Who on Earth would want to coach me?' But as I was coming off an injury and didn't want to get injured again, I built up the courage and contacted Nick. It's been fantastic. He has explained and implemented the concepts around running. As a result, I have made consistent improvement. I know exactly what I have to do and when. I never thought I would be able to run as well as I now can. Recently I completed the Heysen 37 km run, which is further than I ever thought possible. I am now looking forward to tackling the same race again next year and am even considering entering my first 50 km ultra.

## RUSS HANNAH - 100 KM ULTRAMARATHON RUNNER

Before working with Nick at The Ultra Journey, I had entered Ultra Trail Australia and unfortunately had a DNF. I had a low level of clarity on how to train as an ultra runner, limiting the progress of my running. I had no adaptable training structure in place. Since working with Nick, I now have a solid, but malleable system to my training plan that I follow and love. I train with confidence and the improvement just keeps coming. I recently completed my first 100 km ultramarathon and couldn't be happier.

## MARCUS STAKER - ULTRA TRAIL AUSTRALIA SILVER BUCKLE HOLDER AND MILER

I started working with Nick leading into my first 100 km ultra: Ultra Trail Australia. I had been running regularly but still didn't feel ready for the event. Nick provided the knowledge, support and feedback that I needed. He outlined a detailed training plan that guided me every step of the way. I finished the event and claimed the coveted silver belt buckle on my first attempt. I have since been back, set another PB, finished another three 100 km events and even finished my first 100 miler (160 km ultra). I keep improving and setting bigger goals. I just love it.

# A REQUEST

If you have loved *Get Run Fit* it would be most appreciated if you could leave an honest review on the site where you purchased the book. These reviews go a long way to helping others have the confidence to pick up the book and gain the insights you have gained. If you are prepared to do this, we would like to say a massive thank you in advance.

# A REQUEST

[illegible]

# ABOUT THE AUTHOR

Nick Muxlow is the best-selling author of *Journey to Kona* and *Journey to 100,* a high performance endurance coach and education professional. He has a degree in Human Movement and Education. With sixteen years' coaching experience, Nick is driven to help others reach their full potential. Nick currently runs The Run Journey, The Ultra Journey and The Kona Journey, has been featured in industry publications, has partnered with industry brands and speaks regularly online and in person to endurance athletes and professional associations. Nick is well known for allowing his clients to get Run Fit and finish with a smile.

## YOU MAY ALSO BE INTERESTED IN